VOCABULARY
for Achievement

Grade 5

Margaret Ann Richek

GREAT SOURCE
WILMINGTON, MA

Margaret Ann Richek

Professor, College of Education, Northeastern Illinois University; consultant in reading and vocabulary study; author of *The World of Words* (Houghton Mifflin)

Writing and Editing: Maryann Langen, Cara Lieb, Sue Paro

Text Design and Production: Publicom, Inc.

Illustrations: Rita Lascaro and Carol Maglitta

Cover Design: Publicom, Inc.

Cover Photo: Stone/Stuart Westmorland

Acknowledgments

The pronunciation key and the dictionary entries on pages 21-24 and 58-59: Copyright © 1998 by Houghton Mifflin Company. Reproduced by permission from THE AMERICAN HERITAGE CHILDREN'S DICTIONARY.

Thesaurus entries on pages 81 and 84: Copyright © 1997 by Paul Hellweg. Reproduced by permission from THE AMERICAN HERITAGE CHILDREN'S THESAURUS.

Printed in the United States

International Standard Book Number: 0-669-47128-3

1 2 3 4 5 6 7 8 9 10 - POO - 05 04 03 02 01 00

Contents

About This Book iv

PLAYING WITH WORDS

Lesson 1 . . . . .**SKILL LESSON:** synonyms 1
Lesson 2 . . . . .To All Appearances: words about how things look 5
Lesson 3 . . . . .In Character: words about people 9
Lesson 4 . . . . .Picture This: words that tell about settings 13
Lesson 5 . . . . .**REVIEW:** Lessons 1–4 17

WORKING WITH WORDS

Lesson 6 . . . . . **SKILL LESSON:** using the dictionary 21
Lesson 7 . . . . . Just the Right Word: parts of speech 25
Lesson 8 . . . . . Double Duty: words that are both nouns and verbs 29
Lesson 9 . . . . . Same but Different: words with multiple meanings 33
Lesson 10 . . . . . **REVIEW:** Lessons 6–9 37

THINKING ABOUT WORDS

Lesson 11 . . . .**SKILL LESSON:** using context 41
Lesson 12 . . . .Words for a New Nation: words from social studies . 45
Lesson 13 . . . .Making Sense: words from science 49
Lesson 14 . . . .Traditional Tales: words from myths 53
Lesson 15 . . . .**REVIEW:** Lessons 11–14 57

FORMING NEW WORDS

Lesson 16 . . . . . **SKILL LESSON:** prefixes and suffixes 61
Lesson 17 . . . . . Under and Over: prefixes *sub-*, *super-* 65
Lesson 18 . . . . . "Not" Again!: prefixes *in-*, *il-*, *im-* 69
Lesson 19 . . . . . One, Two, Three . . . : prefixes *uni-*, *bi-*, *tri-* 73
Lesson 20 . . . . . **REVIEW:** Lessons 16–19 77

GOING BEYOND WORDS

Lesson 21 . . . .**SKILL LESSON:** using a thesaurus 81
Lesson 22 . . . .Great Advice: proverbs 85
Lesson 23 . . . .It's All Greek: words from Greek 89
Lesson 24 . . . .Good or Bad?: shades of meaning 93
Lesson 25 . . . .**REVIEW:** Lessons 21–24 97

LOOKING INTO WORDS

Lesson 26 . . . . . **SKILL LESSON:** word parts 101
Lesson 27 . . . . . Opposite "Dis-": prefix *dis-* 105
Lesson 28 . . . . . Across the Way: prefix *trans-* 109
Lesson 29 . . . . . Around and Around: word parts *ambi-*, *amphi*, *circu-* 113
Lesson 30 . . . . . **REVIEW:** Lessons 26–29 117

Word List 121

About This Book

That's a Lot of Words!

When you started school, you knew about 5,000 words. By the time you graduate from high school, you will probably know about 60,000 words! How does a person learn all those words? There are two main ways to learn new words: by reading a lot and by studying words.

You are in charge of reading a lot! However, in this book you will learn to study words by learning new words and meanings, understanding that words have different jobs to do (parts of speech), recognizing different forms of words, and using word parts.

Ways to Learn Words

A dictionary and a thesaurus will help you learn new words. For each word listed inside it, a **dictionary** tells the pronunciation, part of speech, and meaning(s). The pronunciation of a word helps you say the word. The part of speech tells whether a word is a noun, verb, adjective, or adverb. A word's definition describes what the word means and the ways it can be used. Sample sentences show you how the word can be used. For each word listed inside a **thesaurus,** there is a list of words that mean about the same thing, or synonyms. Use a thesaurus when you need a really clear, specific word in your writing.

This book will also teach you how to use synonyms, parts of speech and word parts to figure out words. Synonyms are words that mean the same thing as another word. Learning them helps you to use and understand different words. If you can figure out the part of speech of a word, it will help you understand what it means. Knowing the meanings of different word parts, such as prefixes, suffixes, and root words, can also help you figure out the meaning of unfamiliar words.

Be a Word Watcher

As you learn new words *in* this book, look for them *outside* the book. See if you can find the words in other books, newspapers, magazines, on TV, or even on the back of a cereal box. When you find a new word, share it with your class. Maybe you'll be the one to find the most new words this year. Good luck!

PLAYING WITH WORDS

Skill Lesson
synonyms, parts of speech

To write well, you need to be able to move words around, take some out, and put better ones in. In other words, you play with words. The next lessons in this book teach you ways to play with words, as well as describe appearances, personalities, and places.

 SYNONYMS A **synonym** is a word that means the same thing, or almost the same thing, as another word. When we use different synonyms, we change our words, and make our writing better. Read this paragraph and circle the word *nice* each time it is used.

It was a nice day for a picnic. Aneisa had on her nice sun hat. Jason had packed a nice lunch for everybody. We all sat down on a nice blanket and enjoyed the nice weather. When the picnic was over, we all played a nice game of soccer.

You can make the writing more interesting by replacing *nice* with synonyms. Choose the synonym that works best in each sentence below and write it on the line.

It was a **(1)** _____ *(sweet/pleasant)* day for a picnic. Aneisa had on her **(2)** _____ *(beautiful/friendly)* sun hat. Jason had packed a **(3)** _____ *(fun/delicious)* lunch for everybody. We all sat down on a **(4)** _____ *(cozy/polite)* blanket and had a **(5)** _____ *(friendly/tasty)* talk. When the picnic was over, we all played a **(6)** _____ *(beautiful/fun)* game of soccer.

USING SYNONYMS Now try this example, using synonyms for the word *go*. Choose the word that works best in each sentence and write it on the line.

The girls decided to **(1)** _____ *(hike/stroll)* up the mountain. Mindy wanted to **(2)** _____ *(race/continue)* as fast as she could, while Dara preferred to **(3)** _____ *(stroll/race)* more slowly. The two girls worked hard to **(4)** _____ *(run/climb)* all the way to the top. After their hard work, the girls took the time to **(5)** _____ *(march/walk)* around the top to look at the view.

Below are lists of synonyms. Add a synonym of your own that fits with each list. Share your words with a partner.

6. run, hurry, _____

7. kneel, bend, _____

8. kick, knock, _____

9. haul, drag, _____

10. kind, gentle, _____

11. big, immense, _____

12. silly, comical, _____

13. quiet, hushed, _____

14. brilliant, bright, _____

15. throw, fling, _____

PARTS OF SPEECH The part of speech, or the way a word works in a sentence, helps you to understand and use a word. Each word in this book is listed with its part of speech. Let's review some parts of speech now.

A **noun** is a person, animal, place, thing, or idea.

Examples: My <u>brother</u> (person) told me his <u>plan</u> (idea) for making <u>money</u> (thing).

  <u>Roberto</u> (person) walked his <u>dog</u> (animal) in the <u>park</u> (place).

An **adjective** describes a noun.

Examples: Daryl is a <u>likeable</u> boy with an <u>easy</u> manner.

  The <u>busy</u> crew worked quickly to clean the <u>dirty</u> warehouse.

A **verb** is a word for an action or way of being.

Examples: The earth <u>spins</u> on its axis as it <u>orbits</u> the sun (action).
  Anna <u>is</u> tall for her age. (way of being).

An **adverb** describes a verb.

Examples: I will <u>gladly</u> pay you for these yummy muffins!

  The tornado moved <u>slowly</u> across the countryside.

Circle the part of speech of the word in dark type.

1. The Mayan Indians **built** many pyramids.   noun / verb

2. Samuel is a **great** carpenter.   adverb / adjective

3. The student responded **slowly** to the principal's questions.
   adverb / verb

4. Yesterday was the first day of our **vacation**.   noun / adjective

ADJECTIVES Adjectives are words that describe or tell about something. Start a collection of adjectives to use in your writing. Fill in the categories below.

Words That Describe Animals

furry

_____

_____

Words That Describe People

intelligent

_____

_____

Adjectives

Words That Describe Places

hilly

_____

_____

_____

Words That Describe Things

slippery

_____

_____

_____

To All Appearances
words about how things look

A Are you sometimes at a loss for words when you try to describe something you have seen? The words below all describe appearances, or how things look. All the words are adjectives.

a tattered flag

1. **elaborate** (ĭ lăb' ər ĭt)
*Something **elaborate** is complicated and has lots of parts or details.* (adjective)
The **elaborate** birthday cake has seven layers and three fruit fillings.

2. **emaciated** (ĭ mā' shē āt' ĭd)
*An **emaciated** person or animal is very thin from starvation.* (adjective)
The cows were so **emaciated** that we could see the outlines of their ribs.

3. **exquisite** (ĕk' skwĭz ĭt)
*Something **exquisite** is very beautiful and fine.* (adjective)
The **exquisite** box was covered with jewels and tiny gold patterns.

4. **fragile** (frăj' əl)
*Something or someone **fragile** is easily broken or hurt.* (adjective)
The **fragile** crystal glasses broke when they bumped together.

5. **homely** (hōm' lē)
*A **homely** person is ugly or not attractive.* (adjective)
The **homely** baby grew to be a cute little child.

6. **lanky** (lăng' kē)
*A **lanky** person is tall and thin.* (adjective)
The **lanky** teenager was fondly nicknamed "Stringbean."

7. **spotless** (spŏt' lĭs)
*Something **spotless** is very clean.* (adjective)
The **spotless** restaurant kitchen passed the state inspection easily.

8. **tattered** (tăt' ərd)
*Something that is **tattered** is torn, old, and ragged. Tattered often refers to cloth.* (adjective)
The **tattered** flag in the museum had been carried in many battles.

Draw a line between each word and its synonym.

1. fragile   skinny

2. emaciated   raggedy

3. tattered   detailed

4. elaborate   breakable

All the boldfaced words in the passage below tell about appearances in some way. Read the passage. Then answer the questions that follow.

An Aesop's Fable: Don't Count Your Chickens

One summer day long ago, a young woman walked to town, carrying a pail of milk on her head. As she went along, she said to herself, "I have worked hard, but now I can plan my future. When I get to town, I will sell this milk, take the money, and buy a hen. The hen will lay eggs, and I will protect them carefully, because eggs are **fragile**. After the chicks are born, I will feed them well so they won't become **emaciated.** When they are healthy chickens, I can sell them. Soon I will have lots of money. This dress is stained and **tattered.** I will throw it away and buy an **exquisite** new one with lovely bows and ribbons. I'll save it for the first big party in town so it will be **spotless.**

"When I get to the party, all the young men will ask me to dance. But I will choose only the strongest and most handsome. I don't want to dance with anyone who is too tall and **lanky**. And if somebody **homely** asks me, I shall shake my head and say, 'No!'"

The milkmaid tossed her head in the air, and the pail tumbled to the ground, spilling milk all over her. That was the end of the young woman's **elaborate** plans.

The lesson we can learn from this is "Don't count your chickens until they are hatched!"

1. Is the young woman rich or poor? How can you tell?

_____

_____

2. What makes the young woman's plans elaborate?

_____

_____

_____

elaborate
emaciated
exquisite
fragile
homely
lanky
spotless
tattered

C Choose the word from the two choices given that best fits in each sentence. Write the word on the line.

1. My favorite old jeans are _____ and torn.
   (*exquisite/tattered*)

2. Dad wiped the kitchen counter until it was _____.
   (*lanky/spotless*)

3. The wind ripped through the _____ paper kite.
   (*fragile/emaciated*)

4. The _____ rules of the computer game are very difficult to master. (*tattered/elaborate*)

5. When the supply of food runs out, people may become
   _____. (*emaciated/homely*)

D The sentences below can be made more descriptive if you provide a **synonym** to replace the underlined word or words. Write a word from the word list on each line that means about the same as the underlined word(s). Notice that sometimes you will replace two words with one word.

1. A medical laboratory needs to be <u>very clean</u>. _____

2. Something <u>easily breakable</u> must be wrapped carefully.

   _____

3. Some people think that bulldogs are <u>ugly</u>, but I think they're cute.

   _____

4. We made <u>complicated</u> plans to get all 100 children to the picnic.

   _____

5. The small painting had <u>very fine</u> detail. _____

6. Our <u>tall, thin</u> friend towered above us. _____

7. Alicia took the <u>torn, old</u> shirt and made it into a rag.

   _____

8. We felt sorry for the <u>very thin</u> people who couldn't get food after the flood. _____

E Complete each sentence with a word or phrase that makes sense. Some other forms of the vocabulary words are used.

1. You might wear **tattered** clothes to _____ .

2. An **exquisitely** dressed person might be wearing _____

   _____ .

3. **Elaborate** directions can be _____ .

4. A **fragile** vase _____ .

5. If something shines **spotlessly,** it _____

   _____ .

ENRICHMENT WORDS

Here are two more words that you can use to describe appearances.

1. **brawny** (brô' nē) *Someone who is* **brawny** *has well-developed muscles and is strong.* (adjective)

   The **brawny** man lifted weights every day.

2. **lithe** (līth) *Someone who is* **lithe** *moves gracefully.* (adjective)

   The **lithe** gymnast performed a graceful routine on the balance beam.

OFF THE PAGE

Make a chart like the one shown here for at least one of the other words in this lesson. Use the example of *fragile* as a guide.

Things That Are Fragile	Synonyms for Fragile
Glass	Breakable
Butterflies	Delicate
Taco shells	
Old paper	

3

In Character
words about people

happy
funny   smart
young

A The words below all describe a person's character. Think about times you have seen a person be, for example, honorable, shrewd, or frustrated.

1. **desperate** (dĕs' pər ĭt) *To be* **desperate** *is to need or want something so much that you are almost hopeless.* (adjective)
The **desperate** man reached out for the lifeboat to keep from drowning.

2. **frustrated** (frŭs' trā təd) *To be* **frustrated** *is to be discouraged or prevented from reaching a goal.* (adjective)
Mom was **frustrated** in her effort to keep the kitchen floor clean because the baby kept dropping his food.

3. **honorable** (ŏn' ər ə bəl) *An* **honorable** *person has high moral standards and deserves respect.* (adjective)
Cheating on tests is not **honorable** behavior.

4. **ill-informed** (ĭl' ĭn fôrmd') *Someone who is* **ill-informed** *does not have enough information or has the wrong information.* (adjective)
An **ill-informed** citizen will not know how to vote in an election.

5. **odious** (ō' dē əs) *An* **odious** *person or thing causes or deserves hate.* (adjective)
The **odious** ruler put thousands of people in prison.

6. **shrewd** (shrood) *A* **shrewd** *person is clever in useful ways.* (adjective)
A **shrewd** shopper watches the newspapers for sales.

7. **solemn** (sŏl' əm) *To be* **solemn** *is to be serious or grave in manner.* (adjective)
The doctor gave us the bad news with a **solemn** voice.

8. **well-informed** (wĕl' ĭn fôrmd')
Someone who is **well-informed** *has accurate information.* (adjective)
The school's Web site keeps parents **well-informed** about homework.

Draw a line between each word and its synonym.
1. frustrated   hopeless
2. shrewd   good
3. desperate   clever
4. honorable   prevented

All the boldfaced words in the passage below tell about character in some way. Read the passage and answer the questions.

Benjamin O. Davis: Leader of the Tuskegee Airmen

Retired General Benjamin O. Davis looked very **solemn** on the day he was promoted to four-star general. He may have been thinking about his long battle against racial discrimination in the Army. When Davis entered West Point in 1932, he faced constant prejudice there. In an **odious** attempt to make him quit, other students gave him "the silent treatment," refusing to talk to him for four years. Davis was **shrewd** enough to realize that complaints would only bring more trouble. He refused to be **frustrated** in achieving his goals. Instead, he studied hard and graduated near the top of his class.

Davis was **desperate** to be a pilot, but he was rejected until World War II broke out. Many **ill-informed** white officers believed African Americans were not smart enough to fly or brave enough to fight. They were soon proved to be wrong. During World War II, African Americans were trained as pilots at the Tuskegee Institute. In combat, commanded by Davis, the Tuskegee Airmen achieved one of the best records of World War II. Davis's unit shot down more than 200 enemy aircraft. The American bomber crews, **well-informed** about the expertise of the Tuskegee Airmen, nicknamed them "Red-Tail Angels" because the tails of their planes were painted bright red. Not a single American bomber plane protected by Davis's 332nd Fighter Group was ever shot down.

Their outstanding performance was an important reason that the armed forces were integrated shortly after World War II. Davis became a three-star general. Fourteen years after he retired, he was awarded a fourth star because of his **honorable** service in the U.S. Army.

desperate

frustrated

honorable

ill-informed

odious

shrewd

solemn

well-informed

1. What problem did Benjamin O. Davis encounter at West Point? Use a word from the word list to describe the people who caused this problem.

_____

2. Choose a boldfaced word from the passage that best describes Davis. Explain your choice.

_____

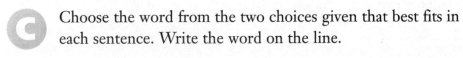 Choose the word from the two choices given that best fits in each sentence. Write the word on the line.

1. When you break something, the *(frustrated/honorable)* thing to do is admit it. _____

2. A graduation is a *(desperate/solemn)*, but happy, occasion.
_____

3. Destroying property is *(odious/well-informed)* behavior.
_____

4. The art dealer gave me a *(shrewd/honorable)* look when he offered me only $20 for the fine painting. _____

5. The mother bear climbed over the fence, *(well-informed/desperate)* to get food for her cubs. _____

D Adding *-ly* to a word makes it an adverb. An adverb describes how something is done or how someone behaves. For example, *desperately* describes someone who behaves in a desperate way. When a word ends in *le*, the *l* and *e* are dropped before *-ly* is added. Use number 1 as a model to fill in the blanks below.

1. desperately = desperate + ly = in a desperate way

2. shrewdly = _____ + ly = _____

3. odiously = _____ + ly = _____

4. honorably = _____ + ly = _____

5. solemnly = _____ + ly = _____

OTHER FORMS

desperately

desperation

frustration

odiously

shrewdly

honorably

solemnly

E Complete each sentence with a phrase that makes sense. Note that some other forms of the vocabulary words are used in the sentences.

1. People feel **frustration** when _____

   _____ .

2. An example of a **solemn** occasion is _____

   _____ .

3. Olivia was **ill-informed** about the weather, so she _____

   _____ .

4. A **shrewd** judge of character _____

   _____ .

5. Someone who behaves **honorably** _____

   _____ .

ENRICHMENT WORDS

Here are two more words that can be used to describe someone's character. Have you seen these words before?

1. **candid** (kăn' dĭd) *A* **candid** *person is open and honest in expressing opinions.* (adjective)
   When Dad gave his **candid** opinion of my paper, I decided to rewrite it.

2. **optimistic** (ŏp' tə mĭs' tĭk) *An* **optimistic** *person views things in the most hopeful and positive way.* (adjective)
   Sue thought she had failed the test, but her mother was more **optimistic**.

OFF THE PAGE

Think of a character in a book that you have read.
Use one or more of the vocabulary words to describe
this character. For example: In the book *Shiloh* by Phyllis Reynolds Naylor,
Shiloh's owner could be described as **odious** because he mistreats dogs.

Picture This
words that tell about setting

A Settings help us to imagine where a story takes place. An adventure story might take place on a lonely mountain or a stormy sea. A science-fiction story might be in outer space. The words below help you to describe settings when you write and to understand them when you read.

lush vegetation

1. **dusk** (dŭsk) **Dusk** *is the time of evening just before darkness.* (noun)
Many state forests close at **dusk** because the woods are dangerous after dark.

2. **gloomy** (gloo' mē) *A* **gloomy** *place is darkened, without much light; a* **gloomy** *person is sad.* (adjective)
Heavy, closed curtains made the room look **gloomy** even on a sunny day.

3. **hamlet** (hăm' lĭt) *A* **hamlet** *is a small town or village.* (noun)
One Indiana **hamlet** has the unusual name of Gnaw Bone.

4. **looming** (loom' ĭng) *Something that is* **looming** *appears to be large and frightening.* (verb)
Tall, dark cliffs were **looming** above us as we pulled our boat to shore.

5. **lush** (lŭsh) *Something* **lush** *is filled with thick, healthy, plentiful plant life.* (adjective)
The rain forests of Hawaii are a **lush** mix of flowers, shrubs, and trees.

6. **plaza** (plăz' ə) *A* **plaza** *is a public square in a town or city or a shopping center.* (noun)
Summer concerts are held on the **plaza** at the center of town.

7. **ravine** (rə vēn') *A* **ravine** *is a deep, narrow gorge or valley.* (noun)
Engineers designed a bridge that crossed the **ravine.**

8. **vegetation** (věj' ĭ tā' shən) **Vegetation** *is plant life.* (noun)
Prairie grass and other natural **vegetation** grow on the Great Plains.

Draw a line between the word and its definition.

1. lush — dark or sad
2. gloomy — early evening
3. vegetation — plentiful
4. dusk — plant life

B All the boldfaced words in the passage below tell about settings in some way. Read the passage and answer the questions.

The Day the Mountain Blew Its Top

In April, 1980, Mount St. Helens volcano had been "sleeping" for more than a hundred years. Its slopes were covered with trees, wildflowers, and other **vegetation.** The mountain was home to birds, bears, elk, and deer. It was a popular recreation area for hikers, boaters, and nature lovers. But on May 18, 1980, the sleeping volcano suddenly awakened and blew its top.

The blast tore the top off the mountain and flattened the tall fir forests on its slopes. Avalanches swept down the mountain, pouring rock, dirt, and mud into the valleys and **ravines** below.

Meanwhile, a huge column of ash and gas was **looming** over the mountain. It was only noon, but it looked like **dusk.** The ash made the sky so dark and **gloomy** that in a small **hamlet** 80 miles away, the streetlights came on in the middle of the day. The ash fell like rain on the shopping **plazas,** houses, streets, and cars of nearby towns.

Back on the mountain, everything had changed. The **lush** forests were gone. The animals were gone. The slopes were now covered with a thick, gray layer of rock and ash. It looked dead. Just a few years later, life began to return to Mount St. Helens. Scientists have been amazed to see how quickly seeds have sprouted, plants have grown, and animals have begun to return.

WORD LIST

dusk

gloomy

hamlet

looming

lush

plaza

ravine

vegetation

1. Why did the streetlights come on in a small hamlet 80 miles away? Use at least two of the boldfaced words in your answer. _____

   _____

   _____

2. List two types of vegetation from the passage. _____

   _____

   _____

C Find the words in the word list that fit each description.

1. Write a word (a noun) that tells a time of the day. _____

2. Write three words (nouns) that name places. _____

   _____

3. Write three words (adjectives) that describe how something looks.

   _____

D Remember that using **synonyms** can make your writing more interesting. Use the words from the word list as synonyms for the underlined word or words below. Remember that you can replace more than one word with a single word.

As I walked through the **(1)** thick forest, I saw the **(2)** little town in the distance. At **(3)** the time of day when the sun was setting, I began to make out the **(4)** public square and the people carrying umbrellas on the **(5)** dark and dreary day.

1. _____

2. _____

3. _____

4. _____

5. _____

E Complete each sentence with a phrase that makes sense. Some other forms of the vocabulary words have been used.

1. **Dusk** is a good time for _____ .

2. A **gloomy** day is _____ .

3. Two huge trees **loom** over _____ .

4. If the **vegetation** is growing **lushly**, _____
_____ .

5. Living in a **hamlet** would be _____

because _____ .

ENRICHMENT WORDS

Here are two more words that can be used to describe a setting.

1. **congested** (kən jĕs' tĭd) *To be* **congested** *is to be overcrowded.*
(adjective)
The road became **congested** because construction crews closed a lane.

2. **dilapidated** (dĭ lăp' ĭ dā' tĭd) *Something that is* **dilapidated** *is in bad condition and needs repair.* (adjective)
The **dilapidated** house had broken windows and peeling paint.

OFF THE PAGE

The details you put in your writing help the reader "see" what you are writing about. Choose one of the settings below. Help your readers "see" the setting by using at least three details in a paragraph to describe it. One detail might be: *All the colors turned to gray as dusk fell on the hamlet.*

1. a hamlet at dusk

2. a gloomy mansion

3. a lush forest

a gloomy mansion

LESSON 5

Review
Lessons 1-4

In this lesson, you will review the words and strategies you have learned in the last four lessons. This will help you to remember them when you read and write.

A MATCHING WORDS AND DEFINITIONS
Choose the word that matches each definition. Write it on the line.

| gloomy | tattered | homely | shrewd | vegetation |

1. darkened or sad _____

2. torn, old, and ragged _____

3. grasses and flowers _____

4. clever _____

5. unattractive, ugly _____

B USING WORDS IN CONTEXT
Use the words in each list to complete each paragraph.

| desperate | dusk | odious | homely | solemn |

As the sun lowered and **(1)** _____ approached, Jonathan became more nervous. He was **(2)** _____ to finish breaking the code before the morning. Bored and annoyed by the **(3)** _____ task, he scribbled out draft after draft of the mysterious coded message. He wrote continuously until his arm ached. Finally, just before dawn, he discovered the key and decoded the letter.

| plaza | looming | ravine | exquisite | solemn |

Adam hiked down the steep **(4)** _____ as the rain fell. Then he saw it. Under a broad leaf were some ancient bones. Next to them was an **(5)** _____ necklace of sparkling stones. He carefully picked it up and took a closer look. His expression became **(6)** _____ when he realized the importance of his discovery.

© Great Source DO NOT COPY

Lesson 5 17

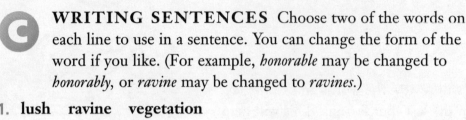 **WRITING SENTENCES** Choose two of the words on each line to use in a sentence. You can change the form of the word if you like. (For example, *honorable* may be changed to *honorably*, or *ravine* may be changed to *ravines*.)

1. lush   ravine   vegetation

_____

_____

2. fragile   tattered   emaciated

_____

_____

3. frustrated   looming   ill-informed

_____

_____

4. honorable   lanky   elaborate

_____

_____

5. elaborate   spotless   exquisite

_____

_____

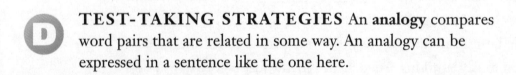 **TEST-TAKING STRATEGIES** An **analogy** compares word pairs that are related in some way. An analogy can be expressed in a sentence like the one here.

Scared is to frightened as tired is to sleepy.

Strategy: To complete an analogy, find out how the words in the first pair are related. The second pair must have the same relationship. *Scared* means about the same as *frightened*, and *tired* means about the same as *sleepy*. Both pairs of words are synonyms. Some analogies are "type of" analogies. For example: A dog is a type of animal, and a maple is a type of tree. The analogy is "Dog is to animal as maple is to tree."

Directions: Choose the word that completes each analogy and write it on the line.

1. Dirty is to filthy as spotless is to _____. *(soap/clean)*

2. Small is to tiny as ripped is to _____. *(tattered/little)*

3. Large is to huge as dark is to _____. *(bright/gloomy)*

4. Honest is to truthful as solemn is to _____.
    (serious/silent)

5. Pretty is to beautiful as unattractive is to _____.
    (lovely/homely)

6. House is to building as hamlet is to _____.
    (town/garage)

7. Lush is to adjective as vegetation is to _____.
    (adverb/noun)

8. Lobby is to indoor space as plaza is to _____.
    (outdoor space/hotel)

9. Piano is to instrument as grass is to _____.
    (flowers/vegetation)

10. Honorable is to adjective as ravine is to _____.
    (verb/noun)

 TEST-TAKING STRATEGIES On a **multiple-choice** test, you have to pick the correct answer out of several choices. Usually two or three answers seem like good choices, but only one answer is correct.

Strategy: Read through each question. Before you search for an answer, think of how you would answer the question. Then look to see if your answer is there. If it is and you are certain it is correct, carefully fill in the bubble next to the answer. If your answer is not there, find the answers that you know are *not* correct. Skip them and focus on the remaining choices. When you decide on your answer, fill in the bubble completely.

Directions: Fill in the bubble next to the word that answers the question.

1. What is another word for *gloomy?*

   (A) nervous   (B) sad   (C) tired   (D) thin

2. How would you describe a tiny, hand-blown glass swan knick-knack?

   (A) lanky   (B) lush   (C) fragile   (D) gloomy

3. What word means about the same as *shrewd?*

   (A) clever   (B) stubborn   (C) sneaky   (D) solemn

4. Which of the following is most likely to be well-informed about high-quality clothing?

   (A) fashion designer   (B) insurance salesperson

   (C) waiter or waitress   (D) doctor or nurse

5. What is another way of saying that someone is extremely thin?

   (A) shrewd   (B) honorable

   (C) exquisite   (D) emaciated

ENRICHMENT WORDS

Draw a line between each Enrichment Word and its definition.

1. brawny   graceful
2. lithe   overcrowded, overfilled
3. optimistic   bad condition, needs repair
4. candid   having muscles, fit
5. dilapidated   seeing things in a good light
6. congested   open and honest

WORKING WITH WORDS

Skill Lesson
Using the Dictionary

The **dictionary** is a good tool to help you improve your vocabulary. It can help you learn new words and understand the many shades of meaning of words you may already know. It can also help you pronounce words correctly.

A **DICTIONARY ENTRIES** People who write dictionaries give a lot of information in a small space. They use shortcuts and abbreviations to keep things brief. The information given for a word in the dictionary is called an **entry.** Look at the entry below.

> [1] [2] [3]
>
> **grandfather** *noun* The father of one's father or mother.
> **grand•fa•ther** (grand' fä'thər) Δ *noun, plural* **grandfathers**
> [4]   [5]

1. **The word.** The entry word is printed in boldface type.

2. **The part of speech.** The part of speech is printed in italic type.

3. **The definition.** This tells what the word means. If there is more than one definition, each will be numbered.

4. **Syllables and pronunciation.** A key shows how to use the symbols. A small mark (') shows which syllable to stress.

5. **Other forms.** Other forms of the word that do not have their own entries may be listed here. The parts of speech may also be included.

This dictionary entry has example sentences. Answer the questions.

> **pretend** *verb* **1.** To put on a false show of: *They pretended illness.*
> **2.** To make believe: *Let's pretend we're famous.*
> **pre•tend** (prĭ tĕnd') Δ *verb* **pretended, pretending**

1. What part of speech is *pretend?* _____

2. How many syllables are in *pretend?* _____

3. How many definitions are there of *pretend?* _____

4. Which syllable is the accented syllable in *pretend?* _____

Name

Date

(B) **PARTS OF SPEECH** Some words can be different **parts of speech,** depending on how they are used. For example, the word *farm* can be a place (noun) as well as an action (verb). Here is what the dictionary entry for *farm* looks like:

farm *noun* **1.** A piece of land on which crops or animals are raised. Δ *verb* **1.** To engage in farming. **2.** To cultivate or produce a crop on **farm** (färm) Δ *noun, plural* **farms** Δ *verb* **farmed, farming**

This sentence shows *farm* used as a **noun.**

My mother lived on a **farm** when she was a little girl.

This sentence shows *farm* used as a **verb.**

In the coming season, the Swansons decided to **farm** rice and beans on their land.

In the dictionary entry below, sample sentences help you understand *promise.*

promise *noun* **1.** A statement that one will do something; vow: *I kept my promise to write home.* **2.** Reason for expecting something, such as future success, excellence, or distinction: *The young dancer shows promise.* Δ *verb* **1.** To make a promise: *I promised to come home early.* **2.** To give reasons for expecting: *The dark clouds promised rain.*
prom•ise (prŏm' ĭs) Δ *noun, plural* **promises** Δ *verb* **promised, promising**

How is the word *promise* used in the following sentences? Write *noun* or *verb* on the line.

1. I **promise** to be at the club meeting tomorrow—no matter what!

_____

2. We can be friends only if you **promise** never to do that again.

_____

3. A **promise** is a **promise.** _____

4. We can still keep our **promise** and help clean up. _____

5. You made a **promise** to me that I will never forget. _____

22 *Working with Words*

© Great Source DO NOT COPY

C **MULTIPLE-MEANING WORDS** Some words have two or more meanings that are quite different from each other. These different meanings can be the same part of speech, or they can be different parts of speech. These kinds of words are called **multiple-meaning words.** For example, the word *trunk* can refer to part of a tree, an elephant, or a car. It can also be a large box.

Here is a dictionary entry for the multiple-meaning word *coach*. Use the entry to fill in the blanks below.

> **coach** *noun* **1.** A large carriage with four wheels that has seats inside and is drawn by horses. **2.** A person who trains or teaches athletes, athletic teams, or performers.
> **coach** (kōch) △ *noun, plural* **coaches**

Read each sentence and decide how the word *coach* is used. Write the number of the correct definition on the line in front of each sentence.

1. _____ The passenger jumped into the **coach** and away they rode.

2. _____ Daisy couldn't help smiling at her **coach** after the big win.

3. _____ After the **coach** pulled into town, the driver fed and watered the horses.

4. _____ "We did our best and that's what counts," said the **coach.**

5. _____ The king and queen waved from the royal **coach.**

Read the dictionary entry for *cow* and answer the questions below.

> **cow** *noun* **1.** The fully grown female of cattle, raised for its milk, meat, and hide. **2.** The female of certain other large mammals, as the elephant. Δ *verb* To frighten with threats.
> **cow** (kou) Δ *noun, plural* **cows** Δ *verb* **cowed**

6. Which noun definition of *cow* is used in the following sentence?

   The walrus **cow** pulled herself out of the water. _____

7. Which noun definition of *cow* is used in the following sentence?

   The **cows** entered the barn at milking time. _____

8. Which part of speech is *cow* in the following sentence?

   The cruel giant **cowed** David with an angry stare.

   _____

9. What part of speech is *cow* in the following sentence?

   Of all our **cows,** Bessy was my father's favorite. _____

COWS

Just the Right Word
different parts of speech

apples   red   easily   pick

A In Lesson 1, you learned about parts of speech. In Lesson 6, you saw how they function in dictionary entries. This lesson will help you to review parts of speech by teaching you two new nouns, verbs, adjectives, and adverbs.

1. **commonplace** (kŏm' ən plās')
Something **commonplace** *is ordinary and uninteresting.* (adjective)
A clover with three leaves is **commonplace,** but a four-leaf clover is very unusual.

2. **enclose** (ĕn klōz') To **enclose** *means to put something in a closed place.* (verb)
My aunt likes to **enclose** money in my birthday card.

3. **magnificent** (măg nĭf' ĭ sənt)
Something **magnificent** *is excellent or wonderful.* (adjective)
Mark McGwire and Sammy Sosa have **magnificent** home run records.

4. **nomad** (nō' măd') *A* **nomad** *is a person who moves from place to place in search of food.* (noun)
A **nomad** who raises cattle in the Himalayas lives in a round tent called a *yurt.*

5. **plea** (plē) *A* **plea** *is an urgent request or call for help.* (noun)
The governor made a special **plea** to the president to provide emergency flood aid.

6. **roam** (rōm) *When we* **roam,** *we wander, or travel around from place to place without a plan.* (verb)
My parents don't allow me to **roam** around the mall by myself.

7. **ruefully** (rōo' fəl ē) **Ruefully** *means done with regret or sorrow.* (adverb) "I wish I hadn't climbed that tree," Lin said **ruefully,** as she rubbed her sprained ankle.

8. **stealthily** (stĕlth' ĭ lē) **Stealthily** *means done in a quiet, secret manner.* (adverb)
The six-year old child **stealthily** opened the cabinet and reached for the cookies.

Draw a line between each vocabulary word and its synonym.

1. nomad   request
2. plea   wonderful
3. magnificent   ordinary
4. roam   travel
5. commonplace   wanderer

Name

Date

B All the boldfaced words in the passage below are either nouns, verbs, adverbs, or adjectives. Read the passage. Then answer the questions that follow.

The Nightingale: A Hans Christian Andersen Story

Long ago, an emperor lived in a **magnificent** palace. Visitors wrote of his great riches, but what they praised most about the country was the sweet song of a plain little gray bird, a nightingale. Curious, the emperor had the nightingale brought to him.

When he heard the nightingale's beautiful song, the emperor decided to keep the bird with him. He **enclosed** her in a gilded cage, and she sang for the emperor as he ate his supper each night.

One day, the emperor was given the gift of a mechanical nightingale. When it was wound up, it sang beautifully. In contrast to the **commonplace** appearance of the real nightingale, the artificial bird was covered with brightly colored jewels. The emperor was so excited about the new bird that he forgot about the gray nightingale. One day, her cage door was left open, and she flew **stealthily** away to live in the nearby forest. When the emperor finally noticed the bird was gone, he became angry and ordered it to leave his country. The nightingale took up the life of a **nomad,** **roaming** from forest to forest in neighboring lands. As for the artificial bird, after a while it just stopped working. There was no more music in the palace.

Years later, the emperor became terribly sick. As he lay in bed, the nightingale suddenly appeared and began to sing. Cheered by the beautiful song, the emperor began to feel better, and at last he sat up in bed. "Dear nightingale, I am so sorry I was angry with you," he said **ruefully.** "You have saved my life. Please stay here with me."

"My dear emperor," replied the nightingale, "I prefer to live free in the forest, but I will return to sing to you every night. I will sing to you of all the good and evil in your kingdom. I have only one **plea** to make: Let no one know that a little bird tells you everything!"

WORD LIST

commonplace

enclose

magnificent

nomad

plea

roam

ruefully

stealthily

1. What is commonplace about the nightingale? What is not?

   _____

2. Use a boldfaced word from the passage in a sentence that describes the nightingale.

   _____

C Fit the right word into each sentence. Write the word on the line.

1. "I broke your favorite pen," Rhonda admitted _____ . *(stealthily/ruefully)*

2. Those high stone walls _____ a beautiful secret garden. *(enclose/roam)*

3. The burglar crept _____ up the stairs. *(ruefully/stealthily)*

4. The _____ view from the top of the mountain made the climb worthwhile. *(magnificent/commonplace)*

5. I would like to _____ the world to learn about different cultures. *(roam/enclose)*

D Classify each word from the word list by its part of speech.

Nouns	Verbs	Adverbs	Adjectives
_____	_____	_____	_____
_____	_____	_____	_____
_____	_____	_____	_____
_____	_____	_____	_____
_____	_____	_____	_____

E Complete each sentence with a phrase that makes sense. Note that some other forms of the vocabulary words have been used.

1. Something you might **enclose** in an envelope is _____

_____ .

2. One **magnificent** view that I have seen is _____

_____ .

3. If you **roam** the world, _____

_____ .

4. You might feel **rueful** about _____

_____ .

5. "Mom," I said **pleadingly**, "may I _____

_____ ?"

ENRICHMENT WORDS

Here are two more words that are examples of different parts of speech.

1. **din** (dĭn) *A* **din** *is a loud, confused, continuous noise.* (noun)
   The **din** of the construction kept us from concentrating on our lesson.

2. **nimble** (nĭm' bəl) *A* **nimble** *person or animal moves quickly and lightly.*
   (adjective)
   You must be **nimble** to be a good gymnast.

OFF THE PAGE

In Exercise C, you classified parts of speech. Now think of two more words for each part of speech and add them to the correct columns. After you list the words, write one sentence with a word from each column.

nimble

Double Duty
words that are both nouns and verbs

wrench

A Some words do double duty. They can be used as either nouns or verbs. For example, we can walk (a verb) or we can take a walk (a noun). Below are double-duty words that may be nouns or verbs.

1. **feast** (fēst) *A* **feast** *is a large meal (noun). When we feast, we eat a large meal (verb).*
   Dad will cook a huge **feast** to celebrate Thanksgiving (noun). We will **feast** on turkey with all the trimmings (verb).

2. **fool** (fool) *A* **fool** *is a person who does not have good sense and is easy to trick (noun). To* **fool** *someone is to trick her or him (verb).*
   She was a **fool** to believe that the moon was made of cheese (noun). It wasn't nice to **fool** her (verb).

3. **guarantee** (găr' ən tē') *A* **guarantee** *is a promise of quality (noun). When we* **guarantee** *something, we promise that something will work as it should (verb).*
   Our new computer came with a **guarantee** that any problem would be fixed without charge (noun). The company will **guarantee** that we will not be charged for repairs (verb).

4. **marvel** (mär' vəl) *A* **marvel** *is something wonderful that surprises us (noun). When we* **marvel** *at something, we express surprise or wonder (verb).*
   The Internet is a **marvel** of modern technology (noun). I **marvel** at how much we can do with it (verb).

5. **scout** (skout) *A* **scout** *is a person sent to find out information (noun). When we* **scout** *we look for something (verb).*
   A **scout** went ahead to find a stream for the campers (noun). We sent Joe ahead to **scout** for water (verb).

6. **shiver** (shǐv' ər) *A* **shiver** *is a small shaking movement we make because we are cold or afraid (noun). When we* **shiver** *we make small shaking movements (verb).*
   A **shiver** went down my back while watching the scary movie (noun). Walking into an air-conditioned store on a hot day makes me **shiver** (verb).

7. **vow** (vou) *A* **vow** *is a solemn promise. (noun) When we* **vow** *we make a solemn promise. (verb).*
   I made a **vow** to my aunt that I would not get lost in the city (noun). She had me **vow** that I would stay by her side at all times (verb).

8. **wrench** (rěnch) *A* **wrench** *is a tool for gripping and turning objects (noun). When we* **wrench** *something, we pull or turn it suddenly (verb).*
   I used a **wrench** to turn the rusted faucet (noun). Don't turn the handle too hard, or you might **wrench** it right off the faucet (verb).

B All of the boldfaced words in the passage below can be either nouns or verbs. Read the passage. Then answer the questions that follow.

Acapulco—A City of Old and New

Beautiful Acapulco is a Mexican town with a long history. For hundreds of years, native peoples lived there peacefully, but in 1530, the Spanish explorer Hernán Cortez **wrenched** control of the city away from them. The city became a major port for ships that transported spices and silks from Asia to Spain. Soon, English and Dutch pirates began to **scout** out the ships to attack them and steal the valuable cargo. So, in 1617, Fort San Diego was built as a place where ships could land safely. The fort is now used as a museum for the many people who visit each year.

Present-day visitors to Acapulco **marvel** at an unusual bronze statue of a patron saint. The statue was placed underwater in the harbor by fishermen to protect people who work on the water. It can be viewed from a glass-bottomed boat. Divers put flowers at the feet of the statue every year on December 12, the day of the saint.

Another marvel, Acapulco's high-diving *clavadistas*, leap from 120-foot cliffs into the water. Their daring dives send **shivers** down the spines of tourists, but the *clavadistas* are not **fools.** They wait for tides to deepen the water before they dive.

After watching the *clavadistas*, you might want to **feast** on some seafood. Then relax and sit in the sun. Acapulco averages 360 days of sunshine and most of the rain falls at night. Although there is no **guarantee,** it will probably be sunny when you are there. At the end of the day, as you enjoy one of the most beautiful sunsets in the world, you may just **vow** to stay in Acapulco forever.

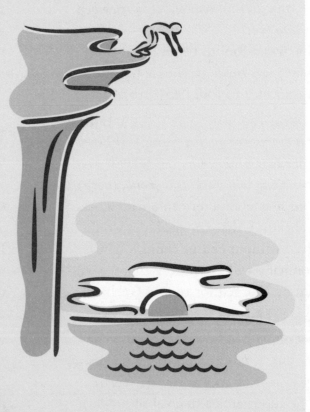

WORD LIST

feast

fool

guarantee

marvel

scout

shiver

vow

wrench

1. Which sights of Acapulco would make you marvel most?

_____

_____

2. List two words used as nouns and two words used as verbs from the passage.

_____

_____

C Choose the word that best fits in each sentence. Write the word on the line. Then write the part of speech.

1. The basketball player was nervous because he knew a *(scout/fool)* was at the game. _____

Part of speech: _____

2. I wish my talkative little sister would take a *(fool/vow)* of silence. _____ Part of speech: _____

3. I *(guarantee/feast)* that you will enjoy that video game. _____ Part of speech: _____

4. The frightening tale sent a *(vow/shiver)* of fear up my spine. _____ Part of speech: _____

5. You will *(fool/marvel)* at the dinosaur exhibit in the museum. _____ Part of speech: _____

D Add the word from the word list that is a **synonym** for the words in each list.

1. look for, search for, find out, explore, _____

2. amazing thing, spectacle, wonderful thing, astonishing thing,

_____

3. trick, deceive, mislead, _____

4. festival, big meal, banquet, celebration, _____

5. tremble, quiver, shake, shudder, _____

OTHER FORMS

foolish

foolishly

marvelous

marvelously

E Complete each sentence with a phrase that makes sense. Note that some other forms of the vocabulary words are used in the sentences.

1. A **foolish** idea can _____

_____ .

2. An example of a **marvelous** event is _____

_____ .

3. I would like to **guarantee** that _____

_____ .

4. You can use a **wrench** to _____

_____ .

5. For a special **feast,** I would serve _____

_____ .

ENRICHMENT WORDS

Here are two more words that can be both a noun and a verb.

1. maneuver (mə n$\overline{oo}$' ver) *To* **maneuver** *is to put a clever plan into action* (verb). *A* **maneuver** *is a skilled or clever step toward a goal* (noun).

   Leo will **maneuver** his bike into the inside track (verb).
   This **maneuver** will help him win the race (noun).

2. rebuke (rĭ by$\overline{oo}$k') *To* **rebuke** *is to blame or criticize in a sharp way* (verb). *A* **rebuke** *is a sharp criticism* (noun).

   Our teacher threatened to **rebuke** us for talking too much (verb).
   After our teacher's **rebuke**, we were quiet (noun).

maneuver

OFF THE PAGE

Many things come with **guarantees.** For example, many computer companies guarantee that the programs they sell will work for a year, or they will replace them for free. Look at home and at school to locate something that comes with a guarantee. Describe the guarantee. Do you think it is a good one?

Same but Different
words with multiple meanings

 A Many English words have more than one meaning. One dictionary lists more than 30 meanings for the common word *run!* All of the words below have at least two meanings.

1. **arm** (ärm) *An* **arm** *is an upper limb of the body connecting the hand and wrist to the shoulder* (noun). *To* **arm** *means to carry or supply with weapons or something that strengthens* (verb).
I carried three towels on my left **arm.** When you go to the beach, **arm** yourself with lots of sunscreen.

2. **charge** (chärj) *A* **charge** *is a price* (noun). *To* **charge** *may mean to ask a price or to rush forward* (verb).
The **charge** for the movie was five dollars. Theaters **charge** five dollars for the movie.

3. **dash** (dăsh) *To* **dash** *means to run quickly; it also means to destroy, especially hopes* (verb).
The racers will **dash** to the finish line. Nothing can **dash** our hopes of winning the championship.

4. **depression** (dĭ prĕsh' ən) *A* **depression** *is a low spot or hollow surrounded by higher places. It is also the state of feeling sad* (noun).
The boy's handprint made a **depression** in the newly poured concrete. After her brother became ill, Amyra went into a **depression.**

5. **gorge** (gôrj) *A* **gorge** *is a narrow valley surrounded by steep walls* (noun). *To* **gorge** *is to stuff oneself with food* (verb).
The hiker slid down the steep, rocky sides of the **gorge.** If you **gorge** yourself with food, you may get sick.

6. **roll** (rōl) *To* **roll** *is to turn over and over* (verb). *A* **roll** *is a continuous series of short beats on a drum* (noun).
We watched the ball **roll** along the sidewalk. The singer was introduced with a dramatic minute-long drum **roll.**

7. **skirt** (skûrt) *A* **skirt** *is a piece of clothing that hangs from the waist* (noun). *To* **skirt** *is to move around the edge of something* (verb).
Tanya prefers to wear pants instead of a **skirt.** We can avoid the traffic if we **skirt** the city.

8. **yarn** (yärn) **Yarn** *is a thick strand of twisted thread used in knitting and weaving. A* **yarn** *is also a long and exaggerated story* (noun).
My mother knit the **yarn** into a warm sweater. Grandfather would often amuse us with a **yarn** about his sailing days.

All the boldfaced words in the passage below have more than one meaning. You can determine the correct meaning by using context. Read the passage. Then answer the questions.

A Paradise in Asia

Explorers in Asia often heard **yarns** of a hidden paradise with a beautiful waterfall located deep within Tibet. Author James Hilton wrote a novel about this paradise, calling it "Shangri-la." Did it really exist? In 1911 and 1924, explorers tried to find Shangri-la and failed. In 1998 the hopes of more explorers were **dashed** when the search was called off because of the accidental death of a team member.

Finally, in 1999, a team headed by National Geographic explorers made a discovery—the Hidden Falls of the Tsangpo. The explorers prepared carefully and went slowly. Past accidents have shown that people cannot **charge** carelessly into wild country and dangerous mountain ranges.

In the Himalayan wilderness, a deep **gorge** leads to another deep gorge. A waterfall in the inner part drops 100 feet into a **depression.** Two men, Ian Baker and Ken Storm, Jr., entered the inner gorge while their companions **skirted** the edge of the first gorge. They **rolled** out traditional mountain-climbing rope to help them go down the last 80 feet to the waterfall. But they were also **armed** with more modern equipment, such as laser range-finders, which they used to measure the depth of the gorge and the height of the waterfall.

Although they had to **dash** back home to report their discovery, the explorers, like the people in James Hilton's story, did not want to leave their Shangri-la.

1. What is the meaning of **gorge** in the passage? How do you know?

_____

2. What is the meaning of **depression** in the passage? How do you know?

_____

WORD LIST

arm

charge

dash

depression

gorge

roll

skirt

yarn

 Write the word from the word list that can be used as a **synonym** for each underlined word or phrase.

1. I'm just going to <u>run quickly</u> to the corner store to buy some milk.

   _____

2. After eating take-out food for two weeks, I wanted to <u>stuff</u> myself on Mom's cooking.   _____

3. "We don't <u>ask a price</u> for a refill on soda," said the waiter.

   _____

4. Building a bridge across a <u>deep valley</u> takes great engineering skill.

   _____

5. The stray moose had to be calmed down when he began to <u>rush forward</u> toward the crowd. _____

D Complete the crossword puzzle, using words from the word box.

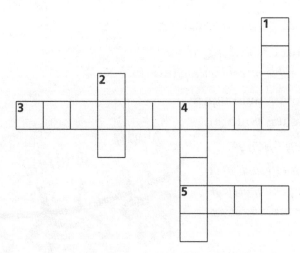

Across

3. sadness; hollow
5. turn over and over; drum beat

Down

1. tale; thread
2. supply with weapons; limb
4. walk around something; clothing

OTHER FORMS

dashed

disarm

engorge

unarmed

unroll

E Complete each sentence with a phrase that makes sense. Some other forms of the vocabulary words are used.

1. A **gorge** looks like _____

_____ .

2. When your hopes are **dashed,** _____

_____ .

3. People who are **unarmed** do not have _____

_____ .

4. Something made out of **yarn** is _____

_____ .

5. An example of something that you can **unroll** is _____

_____ .

ENRICHMENT WORDS

Here are two more words that have more than one meaning.

1. **counter** (koun' tər) *When you* **counter** *something, you act against it* (verb). *A* **counter** *is a long table or cabinet top* (noun).

   An aspirin may **counter** the pain from a mild injury. People often cut vegetables on a kitchen **counter.**

2. **medium** (mē' dē əm) **Medium** *is a point in the middle, between two extremes, such as small and large* (adjective). *A* **medium** *(plural* **media***) is a material or technique used for producing art or communication* (noun).

   We bought **medium** size eggs, rather than large ones. Watercolor is a popular **medium** for children's art.

OFF THE PAGE

Charge, dash, and **roll** have even more meanings than are listed in this lesson. Use a dictionary to find out one other meaning for each word. Write sentences or draw pictures that explain the words so that you can tell someone another meaning and the part of speech.

Review
Lessons 6-9

In this lesson, you will review the words and strategies you have learned in the last four lessons. This will help you to remember them when you read and write.

A **MATCHING WORDS AND DEFINITIONS**
Write the word from the box that matches each definition.

| plea marvel vow magnificent enclose arm |

1. excellent or wonderful _____

2. an urgent request or call for help _____

3. a solemn promise _____

4. to carry or supply with weapons _____

5. something wonderful and surprising _____

6. put inside something _____

B **USING WORDS IN CONTEXT** Use the words in each box to complete the paragraphs.

| guarantee vowed stealthily fool yarns |

The politician was a skilled campaigner. He had a way of making everyone happy. He told amusing **(1)** _____ about his childhood and made people laugh. Then he told sad stories of poor people, and the crowd listened with solemn faces. But he **(2)** _____ avoided making any promises. He would not **(3)** _____ anything to us. When I heard him, I **(4)** _____ to myself that I would never be like him. I would not try to **(5)** _____ people into voting for me. I would be an honest and straightforward politician.

| shiver | commonplace | gorge | dash | feast |

The sights when you swim underwater can be a
(6) _____ for the eyes. It is (7) _____
to see exquisite coral formations. Schools of brightly colored fish
(8) _____ quickly from place to place. A friend of mine
once found herself so close to an octopus it made her (9) _____
with excitement! She half expected the strange creature to start speaking to
her, as if she were in a science-fiction movie. Instead, it seemed to ignore
her and disappeared into a deep (10) _____ far below.

C   **PARTS OF SPEECH** Write *noun* or *verb* to tell the part of
speech of the boldfaced word in each sentence.

1. It has been about 65 million years since dinosaurs **roamed** the earth.

   _____

2. The new car came with a **guarantee** for parts and labor.

   _____

3. Stacey was so upset about losing the gardening competition, she began
   to **wrench** the plants from the ground. _____

4. The farmer decided to **enclose** the pasture with a fence.

   _____

5. Because of the rocky ground, we had to **scout** for a flat place to pitch
   our tents. _____

6. Bedouins are **nomads** who live in the deserts of the Middle East and
   Northern Africa. _____

D MULTIPLE-MEANING WORDS Circle the correct part of speech and definition for the boldfaced word.

1. I couldn't believe he had the nerve to **charge** five dollars for a hot dog!

   verb: ask a price   *noun:* the price of something

2. The ancient site had been such a popular spot for grinding grain that a **depression** had formed in the rock.

   noun: low spot or hollow   *noun:* the state of feeling sad

3. The stunned crowd stood silently watching the truckload of pipes **roll** down Main Street.

   noun: continuous series of short beats on a drum

   verb: turn over and over

4. According to family legend, the blanket was knitted from the finest **yarn** available.

   noun: thick strand of thread   *noun:* exaggerated story

5. While the hikers ate their lunch by the edge of the **gorge,** they were treated to a breathtaking view.

   noun: steep, rocky valley   *verb:* stuff oneself with food

6. When she lost the race, Sylvia's hopes of ever getting to the district finals were **dashed.**

   verb: ran quickly   *verb:* destroyed

7. To keep our feet dry, we tried to **skirt** the edge of the puddle.

   verb: step around   *noun:* clothing

8. Mom and Dad keep a **wrench** in the toolkit in the car, just in case.

   verb: pull suddenly   *noun:* a tool

TEST-TAKING STRATEGIES (Analogies) Remember that an **analogy** compares word pairs that are related in some way. Analogies also appear on many tests, so practicing them will make you a better test taker.

Strategy: The key to solving analogies is figuring out how the words are related. Three kinds of relationships are shown in the analogies below.

1. **kind, or type, of** (*soccer* is a kind of *sport*)
2. **synonym** (*scared* is a synonym for *frightened*)
3. **antonym** (*ill* is an antonym of *healthy*)

Directions: Choose the word that completes each analogy and write it on the line.

1. Ruefully is to regretfully as happily is to _____ .
   gladly/sadly

2. Intelligent is to smart as commonplace is to _____ .
   foolish/ordinary

3. Hamlet is to village as meal is to _____ . *feast/eat*

4. Closed is to open as terrible is to _____ .
   magnificent/emaciated

5. Green is to color as gorge is to _____ . *valley/plaza*

ENRICHMENT WORDS

Draw a line between each Enrichment Word and its definition.

1. nimble   point in the middle/material for producing art
2. din   act against/long table top
3. rebuke   blame or criticize/sharp criticism
4. maneuver   moving quickly and lightly
5. counter   loud continuous noise
6. medium   clever step toward a goal/steer around

THINKING WITH WORDS

Skill Lesson
using context

follicles

dermis

When you come across an unfamiliar word in your reading, you can often figure out its meaning by using the **context**. A word's context is the group of words and sentences around it.

 SENTENCE CONTEXT When you use context clues, you combine your reading, your knowledge of how words and sentences work, and your general knowledge to figure out the meaning of an unknown word. Suppose you are reading about the human body and come across this sentence:

Hairs grow from **follicles** in the **dermis,** the inner, deeper layer of the skin.

You can use common sense to figure out a lot about the words that may be unfamiliar, *follicles* and *dermis*. In fact, the word *dermis* is defined in the sentence.

1. Write the words that you can use to figure out what *dermis* means. Then write a meaning for the word. _____

   _____

2. Now you can use the meaning of the word *dermis* to help you with *follicle*. Think about what *dermis* means and what you already know about hair from your own experience. What do you think follicles are?

   _____

This was all done by thinking with words, or using context. You did not have to interrupt your reading to look up the new words in the dictionary. If you wish, you can take the time to add to your understanding of the new words by using a dictionary at the end of your reading.

SUBSTITUTION CONTEXT CLUES Rereading the example sentence on page 41 and substituting the phrase *tiny holes* for *follicles* helped you make sense of the sentence. When you did this, you were using **substitution context clues.** This is when you substitute another word or phrase for the unknown word to help you make sense of text. Here is another example in which the substitution method of context clues can help you figure out unfamiliar words.

As a volcano erupts, the hot, **molten** rock flows down the mountainside.

Since the rock is hot and flows, the word *melted* would be a good substitute for *molten*: As the volcano erupts, the hot, **melted** rock flows down the mountainside.

Now you try. Choose the best substitute for the boldfaced word in the sentences. Circle your answer.

1. The store owner appeared to be **prosperous,** with her diamond necklace and designer clothing.   tasteful   successful

2. News traveled from city to city throughout the **realm** that the golden knight had defeated the enemy.   house   kingdom

3. "Alas," said the dying hero. "I am a mere **mortal** and cannot live forever."   human   injury

4. Because she had delayed calling the doctor, the pain had worsened and become quite **acute.**   sharp   recent

5. The exhausted dog was so sound asleep that he was not even **responsive** to the loud noise of the crowd.   reacting   dreaming

realm

DEFINING CONTEXT CLUES If you look back at the example sentence on page 41, you will see that you used another kind of context clue to help you figure out the meaning of the word *dermis*. In that case, the word was defined for you right in the sentence. This is called a **defining context clue.**

One clue to readers that a definition follows the word is the use of commas, as in the example with *dermis*. The defining clue is the phrase "the inner, deeper layer of the skin," which follows the comma after *dermis*. Other signs of a defining context clue are the use of parentheses, dashes, or words such as *or*.

> The teenager tried to **emulate** *(or imitate)* the movie star's appearance.
>
> The teenager tried to **emulate**—*or imitate*—the movie star's appearance.
>
> The teenager tried to **emulate**, *or imitate*, the movie star's appearance.

Now try these examples. Underline the words in the sentence that tell you the meaning of the boldfaced word. Then write the word's definition.

1. Sharks have a reputation of being fierce **predators,** animals that hunt and feed on other animals.

   A predator is _____ .

2. The world's largest **crustacean** (shellfish) is the giant spider crab, which has a leg span of almost 13 feet.

   A crustacean is _____ .

3. In the Middle Ages, knights would have tournaments in which one would try to **dislodge** another knight from his horse with a **lance;** that is to say, the knights tried to knock each other off their horses using long spears.

   To dislodge is _____ .

   A lance is _____ .

D **OPPOSITE CONTEXT CLUES** There is another kind of context clue to help you figure out the meaning of an unfamiliar word. Sometimes writers help you know what something means by telling you what it does <u>not</u> mean. This is called an **opposite context clue.** Be on the lookout for words such as *not, no, rather, but,* and *however* to help you find opposite context clues. Here are some examples:

Our business was <u>not</u> **inundated** with calls on our first day, <u>but</u> we did receive one or two requests. (Since one or two calls is <u>not</u> being inundated, you can figure out that *inundated* must mean getting a lot of something.)

I would <u>rather</u> be **jubilant** than depressed. (The word *rather* lets you know that *jubilant* means *happy*, the opposite of *depressed*.)

Roberto thought the fund raiser would be quite **lucrative,** <u>but</u> the other team members thought it wouldn't raise any money. (The word *but* tells you that Roberto's opinion was the opposite of the rest of the team's. *Lucrative* must mean raising a lot of money.)

Write the letter of the word or phrase that means about the same as the boldfaced word.

vertebrates

1. At first the opposing team seemed **invincible,** but in the end, they were easily beaten. _____
   a. unbeatable   **b.** snobby   **c.** unpredictable

2. The animal was not a **vertebrate** because it had no backbone. _____
   a. an animal with ears
   b. an animal with four legs
   c. an animal with a spine

3. Senator Goldstein had not been elected to the Senate; rather he had been **appointed** by the governor when the former senator died. _____
   a. elected by a majority of voters
   b. assigned or chosen by someone else
   c. elected by a committee

4. The **rebellion** was not a success. At the end of the fighting, conditions remained as they had been. _____
   a. violent uprising   **b.** quiet complaint   **c.** calm cooperation

Words for a New Nation
words from social studies

 This lesson presents words you will often find when you study history or read historical fiction. Many relate to the time of the American Revolutionary war, but you will also find them in books dealing with other eras or about government.

1. **abolish** (ə bŏl' ĭsh) *To* **abolish** *is to end rules, laws, or something in government.* (verb)
Colonists wanted the king to **abolish** the tax on tea.

2. **appointed** (ə poin' tĭd) *A person who is* **appointed** *to a job is chosen or assigned by someone else.* (adjective)
Sent by the King of England, **appointed** governors served the American colonies.

3. **apprentice** (ə prĕn' tĭs) *An* **apprentice** *is a person who learns to do a job by working with someone skilled in the job.* (noun)
In colonial times, a young boy served as an **apprentice** in candle making, carpentry, or printing.

4. **carriage** (kăr' ĭj) *A* **carriage** *is a wagon, usually pulled by horses, used to carry people.* (noun)
The **carriage** carried passengers from Houston to Austin in three days.

5. **elected** (ĭ lĕk' tĭd) *A person who is* **elected** *is chosen by vote for a job or office.* (adjective)
Elected members of the U.S. Congress are chosen by their districts.

6. **prosperous** (prŏs' pər əs) *A* **prosperous** *person has wealth, or money, and is successful.* (adjective)
The store owner started out poor but became **prosperous**.

7. **rebellion** (rĭ bĕl' yən) *A* **rebellion**, *or uprising, takes place when people fight against their own government.* (noun)
American colonists threw chests of tea into Boston Harbor as a **rebellion** against high taxes.

8. **representative** (rĕp' rĭ zĕn' tə tĭv) *A* **representative** *is a person elected or chosen to act for a group of people.* (noun)
Our class chose a **representative** to serve on the school council.

Draw a line between each vocabulary word and its definition.

1. appointed   uprising
2. rebellion   wealthy
3. abolish   get rid of
4. prosperous   assigned

The boldfaced words in the passage below are connected
to the time of the American Revolution. Read the passage.
Then answer the questions that follow.

Benjamin Franklin: A Man of Many Talents

"He snatched the lightning from the skies," said someone about Benjamin Franklin. Born in 1706, Franklin was the 15th of 17 children. At age ten, he began to work for his brother as a printer's **apprentice.**

When he was 17, Franklin decided to start a new life in Philadelphia. There he published *Poor Richard's Almanac*, a collection of practical wisdom that made him **prosperous.** Franklin was **appointed** Deputy Postmaster of Philadelphia. He also invented the lightning rod.

After he was **elected** to the Pennsylvania Assembly, Franklin was sent to England as a **representative** of the American colonies. In 1775, he returned to Philadelphia to find that open **rebellion** against Britain had begun. Franklin became caught up in the American Revolution. He went to Canada in an attempt to get support for the Revolution. The trip was a failure, but on his return, Franklin was asked to take part in writing the Declaration of Independence. Then he traveled to France to get support for the revolutionary army.

When he returned in 1785, the war had been won and British rule had been **abolished.** But the colonies needed a government of their own. Franklin, then 81, was asked to attend the Constitutional Convention that would establish this government. Too weak to travel by **carriage,** he was carried to and from the convention in a special chair.

1. What is one of Franklin's most important accomplishments? Tell why you think so.

_____

_____

2. All of the following words describe Franklin in some way. Choose two of the words and explain your choices.

   apprentice   elected   rebellion   representative

_____

_____

WORD LIST

abolish

appointed

apprentice

carriage

elected

prosperous

rebellion

representative

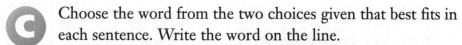 Choose the word from the two choices given that best fits in each sentence. Write the word on the line.

1. One job of the president is to fill *(abolished/appointed)* positions. _____

2. The newly *(elected/abolished)* president of the student council won by a huge majority of students. _____

3. Some American colonists did not want to join in the *(carriage/rebellion)* against British rule. _____

4. Our school sent a *(rebellion/representative)* to speak to the school board about a new gym. _____

5. By going to business school, Tim hoped to become a *(prosperous/apprentice)* business owner. _____

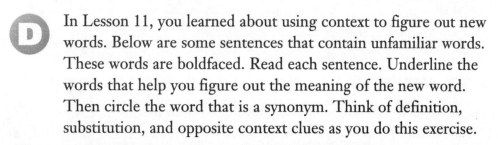 In Lesson 11, you learned about using context to figure out new words. Below are some sentences that contain unfamiliar words. These words are boldfaced. Read each sentence. Underline the words that help you figure out the meaning of the new word. Then circle the word that is a synonym. Think of definition, substitution, and opposite context clues as you do this exercise.

1. The **flourishing** businesswoman bought a huge boat.

   prosperous   *elected*

2. The **conveyance,** or wagon, was on display in the museum.

   carriage   *rebellion*

3. The people did not elect the superintendent of education; it was an **assigned** job.   *appointed*   *prosperous*

4. The school board did not continue the job of assistant principal, but rather they **terminated** it.   *rebellion*   *abolished*

5. The **novice,** a learner, was just out of school.

   apprentice   *prosperous*

OTHER FORMS

appointment
apprenticeship
election
prosperity
rebel
rebellious
represent

 Complete each sentence with a phrase that makes sense. Note that some other forms of the vocabulary words are used in the sentences.

1. A **rebellious** attitude can lead to _____

   _____ .

2. I would like to **abolish** _____

   _____ .

3. A sign of **prosperity** is _____

   _____ .

4. An **apprenticeship** would be helpful to learn about _____

   _____ .

5. A **carriage** is used to _____

   _____ .

ENRICHMENT WORDS

Here are two more words that will help you read about government, history, and historical fiction.

1. **convene** (kən vēn') *To* **convene** *is to assemble together for an official purpose.*

   Leaders of the new American nation **convened** the Continental Congress to discuss forming a government.

2. **proclamation** (prok' lə mā' shən) *A* **proclamation** *is a public announcement or statement.* (noun)

   The Declaration of Independence was a **proclamation** of freedom from British rule.

OFF THE PAGE

In most states the governor appoints a state superintendent of education to set school policy. Do you feel that this should be an **elected** or an **appointed** position? Explain your answer.

LESSON
13

Making Sense
words from science

a vertebrate

A Science teaches us much about the animal world. The words in this lesson will help you to describe animals and the senses that they use to see, hear, smell, taste, and feel their world.

1. **acute** (ə kyo͞ot') *Something* **acute** *is very sensitive and sharp.* (adjective)
The eagle's **acute** vision allows it to see small animals from miles away.

2. **auditory** (ŏ' dĭ tôr' ē) **Auditory** *refers to the sense of hearing.* (adjective)
Listening to music is an **auditory** experience.

3. **olfactory** (ŏl făk' tə rē) **Olfactory** *refers to the sense of smell.* (adjective)
Even though snakes don't see or hear very well, they have an excellent **olfactory** sense.

4. **predator** (prĕd' ə tər) *A* **predator** *is an animal that hunts and feeds on other animals.* (noun)
Sharks are **predators** that feed on smaller fish.

5. **responsive** (rĭ spŏn' sĭv) *Something that is* **responsive** *reacts to something else.* (adjective)
A cat's eyes are **responsive** to light; the pupils become smaller in bright light.

6. **species** (spē' shēz) *A* **species** *is a group of similar animals or plants that can produce young.* (noun)
All breeds of dogs belong to the same **species.**

7. **tactile** (tăk' təl) **Tactile** *refers to the sense of touch.* (adjective)
The antenna is the **tactile** organ an ant uses to feel its world.

8. **vertebrate** (vûr' tə brĭt) *A* **vertebrate** *is an animal with a backbone.* (noun)
Vertebrates include fish, amphibians, reptiles, birds, and mammals.

Draw a line between each vocabulary word and its definition.

1.	species	sense of hearing
2.	auditory	sharp
3.	tactile	sense of touch
4.	acute	group of similar animals
5.	responsive	an animal with a backbone
6.	vertebrate	reactive
7.	olfactory	sense of hearing
8.	auditory	sense of smell

All the boldfaced words in the passage below relate to science. Read the passage. Then answer the questions that follow.

The Five Senses of Whales

How does a whale see, hear, taste, feel, and smell? Like human beings, whales are **vertebrates** and mammals. But, of course, a whale's senses must be specially adapted to life in water.

A whale's eyes are placed on the sides of its head, so each eye sees different things. Because deep water is dark, the whale's eyes let in as much light as possible. Some whales can widen their eyes, showing the white part, to express anger. Whales have small **olfactory** organs; their blowholes are used only for breathing, not smelling. Like our **species,** whales have taste buds on their tongues.

Whales have a **tactile** sense and they like to be rubbed gently. Although they are **predators** of other animals, whales show affection to each other. A baby whale is **responsive** to the comforting feel of a mother's body.

The whale's most **acute** sense is its hearing. Whales communicate using low moans, squeals, grunts, whistles, and cries. The sounds of the blue whale can travel sixty miles!

Whales also listen to their own voices to get information. In "echolocation," whales make sounds so high that humans cannot hear them. These sounds bounce, or echo, off objects in the ocean. The sounds enable whales to locate food and swim without bumping into caves and reefs. A whale seems to gather as much information from its **auditory** sense as a human being gathers from vision.

Amazingly, whales are always using their senses. Only one half of a whale's brain sleeps at a time, while the other half is sensing the outside world.

WORD LIST

acute
auditory
olfactory
predator
responsive
species
tactile
vertebrate

1. What is the most surprising thing you learned about whales? Explain.

_____

2. Explain how each of the following terms relates to the senses.

   olfactory _____

   tactile _____

   auditory _____

C Choose the word from the two choices given that best fits in each sentence. Write the word on the line.

1. A well-trained horse is *(responsive/auditory)* to its trainer's commands.
_____

2. In science we are going to study animals that have backbones, or *(predators/vertebrates)*. _____

3. My dad grows only local *(species/vertebrates)* of plants in his garden. _____

4. Coyotes are *(predators/species)* that hunt and feed on smaller animals, such as rodents. _____

5. The bobcat's *(tactile/acute)* hearing picked up the soft rustle of a mouse in the underbrush. _____

D Think about the words **olfactory, tactile,** and **auditory.** Then write each word above the column where it fits best. Finally, add three words that fit to the bottom part of each box.

_____	_____	_____
noise	scent	rough
sounds	smell	touch
screech	odor	slimy

OTHER FORMS

| acuity |
| auditorium |
| invertebrate |
| predatory |
| response |
| unresponsive |

E Complete each sentence with a phrase that makes sense. Some other forms of the vocabulary words are used.

1. An example of a **predator** is _____ .

2. An example of an **invertebrate** is _____ .

3. A dangerous **species** on earth is _____ .

4. If you lose your **olfactory** sense, _____

_____ .

5. You could go to an **auditorium** to _____

_____ .

ENRICHMENT WORDS

Here are two more words that you might use in science.

1. **dormant** (dôr' mənt) *A plant or animal that is* **dormant** *is not active for a period of time.* (adjective)

   Many plants go into a **dormant** state when they do not have enough water.

2. **nutritious** (noo trĭsh' əs) *A food that is* **nutritious** *gives us the nutrients, or substances, needed for life, growth, and health.*

   Carrots and broccoli are **nutritious** because they contain lots of vitamins.

OFF THE PAGE

Your senses alert you to both pleasant and unpleasant things. For example, a rose has a pleasant smell, or olfactory sensation. However, a skunk gives off an unpleasant smell. Pick one of the senses (olfactory, auditory, tactile) and list three pleasant and three unpleasant sensations.

LESSON 14

Traditional Tales
words from myths

A Ancient peoples needed to explain the forces of nature that they could not understand. Why did the sun rise and set? Why did the seasons change? To do this, they invented traditional tales called "myths." The words in this lesson relate to myths.

1. **myth** (mĭth) *A* **myth** *is a traditional legend or story about ancestors, heroes, or gods.* (noun)
    In one Greek **myth,** Icarus tried to fly, but the sun melted his wax wings.

2. **fate** (fāt) **Fate** *is an outcome that has been decided upon ahead of time.* (noun)
    In Greek myth, the **fate** of Sisyphus was to forever roll a stone up a hill, only to have it tumble down again.

3. **immortal** (ĭ môr' tl) *Someone who is* **immortal** *lives forever.* (adjective)
    According to Greek myth, gods like Zeus, Athena, and Apollo were **immortal.**

4. **invincible** (ĭn vĭn' sə bəl) *Someone who is* **invincible** *cannot be defeated.* (adjective)
    According to Greek myth, the warrior Achilles was **invincible,** except in one weak spot—his heel.

5. **mortal** (môr' tl) *Someone who is* **mortal** *is human and cannot live forever.* (adjective)
    In Greek mythology, a **mortal** being, Psyche, loved an immortal god, Eros.

6. **psyche** (sī' kē) *A* **psyche** *is a person's state of mind or spirit.* (noun)
    Matthew didn't let his defeat in the swimming finals affect his **psyche.**

7. **realm** (rĕlm) *A* **realm** *is the land, or kingdom, that a king or queen rules.* (noun)
    In Greek myth, the underworld was the **realm** of the god Hades.

8. **timeless** (tīm' lĭs) *Something* **timeless** *is not affected by time and seems to last forever.* (adjective)
    Myths have a **timeless** quality because people behaved much the same then as now.

Draw a line between each vocabulary word and its definition.

1. mortal   state of mind
2. psyche   outcome decided already
3. myth   human
4. fate   traditional story
5. immortal   unbeatable
6. invincible   living forever

All the boldfaced words in the passage below are related to myths. Read the passage. Then answer the questions that follow.

Persephone and Demeter

Like most cultures, the Ancient Greeks had a tradition of **myths,** or stories, that explained the forces of nature. The myths centered on gods who had all the faults of **mortal** human beings. People have been repeating these myths for more than 2,500 years, which proves their **timeless** appeal.

The myth of how winter came to be shows how the **immortal** gods, acting out of revenge and jealousy, influenced the **fate** of humans. Long ago, the earth was a green paradise warmed all year by Demeter, the goddess of agriculture. Demeter had a beautiful daughter named Persephone. One day, Persephone wandered away to explore a field of flowers. Unfortunately, Hades, god of the underworld, happened to be visiting the earth. When he saw Persephone, he fell in love with her and carried her off to his underworld **realm** to be his bride.

Demeter was desperate to get her daughter back. Her **psyche** was so affected that she forgot to warm the world. Soon it fell into endless winter. Finally, she spoke to Zeus, king of the gods. Zeus was **invincible,** and all of the gods would follow his orders. Demeter complained to Zeus, and he agreed to let Persephone return home, but only if she had not eaten anything.

Unfortunately, Persephone had eaten six seeds. So Demeter and Hades struck a deal. Persephone would stay with her mother for six months and with Hades for six months. When Persephone is with her mother, Demeter happily warms the earth, and we have summer. When Persephone is with Hades, Demeter is sad and we have winter.

1. Choose two of the following vocabulary words. Write a sentence for each word that explains how it relates to Demeter.

    fate   myth   immortal   realm

    _____

    _____

2. How can you tell from the context what *myth* means?

    _____

    _____

WORD LIST

myth

fate

immortal

invincible

mortal

psyche

realm

timeless

C Choose the word from the two choices given that best fits in each sentence. Write the word on the line.

1. The ancient _____ (*realm/myth*) explained the origin of the sun.

2. The book *Tuck Everlasting* deals with _____ (*immortals/mortals*) who do not grow old and die.

3. The beauty of the ancient Greek statue is _____ (*invincible/timeless*), and it is still lovely even after 4000 years.

4. My _____ (*realm/psyche*) was helped by the many compliments I received.

5. Sometimes things just seem to happen because of _____ (*psyche/fate*) and are beyond our control.

D In Lesson 11, you learned about using context to figure out new words. Below are some sentences that contain unfamiliar words. These words are boldfaced. Read each sentence. Underline the words that help you figure out the meaning of the new word. Then circle the word that is a synonym. Think of definition, substitution, and opposite context clues as you do this exercise.

1. The **impregnable** fort did not fall to the enemy.
   invincible   immortal

2. Human beings cannot always decide their own **karma.**
   fate   timeless

3. The **domain** of the Spanish king once included much of South America.   *realm   mortal*

4. The **fabrications** told by the ancient Norse people explained the creation of the world.   *mortals   myths*

5. The story of Cinderella seems **eternal** because it has been told in different versions for thousands of years.   *timeless   invincible*

OTHER FORMS

mythology

fateful

immortality

mortality

timelessness

E Complete each sentence with a phrase that makes sense. Note that some other forms of the vocabulary words are used in the sentences.

1. A character in Greek **mythology** is _____ .

2. If I were **immortal,** _____ .

3. Zeus wanted everyone in his **realm** to _____ .

4. I wonder if it is my **fate** to _____

_____ .

5. Something that affects my **psyche** is _____

_____ .

ENRICHMENT WORDS

Here are two more words that you can use to talk about mythology.

1. **deity** (dē' ĭ tē) *A* **deity** *is a god or goddess.* (noun)

   According to Greek myth, Neptune was the **deity** who ruled the sea.

2. **Olympian** (ō lĭm' pē ən) **Olympian** *refers to Mount Olympus, where the Greek gods were said to have lived. It can also mean anything that is very powerful or godlike. This word is related to the Olympic games, which were started by the Ancient Greeks to honor their gods.* (adjective)

   The Greek god Zeus had **Olympian** powers because he ruled heaven and earth.

OFF THE PAGE

The stories about superheroes that appear in comics, television, and movies might be called modern **myths.** Describe your favorite superheroes. In what way do stories about them seem like myths?

In this lesson, you will review the words and skills you have learned in the last four lessons. This will help you to remember them.

A MATCHING WORDS AND DEFINITIONS
Write the word from the box that matches each definition.

invincible	fate	appointed	species	elected	immortal	rebellion	realm

1. kingdom _____

2. outcome decided ahead of time _____

3. living forever _____

4. chosen by a vote _____

5. group of similar living things _____

6. assigned or chosen by someone _____

7. not able to be defeated _____

8. uprising against the government _____

B USING WORDS IN CONTEXT Use the words in the box to complete the paragraph.

acute	apprentice	myth	carriage	prosperous	timeless

There is a **(1)** _____ in my family about how my ancestors came to settle on this land. According to the story, my great-great-grandparents came to this area long ago. Everything they owned was on one horse-drawn **(2)** _____ . After settling here, their young son, my great-grandfather became an **(3)** _____ to a local carpenter. Eventually he started his own business and became quite **(4)** _____ . Imagine how disappointed I was to learn that the story was all made up. The truth is that my parents moved to this town shortly before I was born!

DEFINITIONS Write the correct word from the box to answer each question.

| representative | abolish | realm | vertebrate | acute | responsive |

1. Which word best describes a very good sense of smell?

   _____

2. Which word describes human beings, whales, mice, and lions?

   _____

3. Which word tells about reacting to something? _____

4. Which word describes the land a king or queen rules?

   _____

5. Which word would you use if you wanted to get rid of something?

   _____

6. Whom might you vote for? _____

D **USING CONTEXT** Each dictionary entry has several meanings. Use the sentence context to decide which meaning is correct. Then write the part of speech (noun, verb, or adjective) and the number of the correct definition.

vital *adjective* **1.** Of or relating to life: *The heart is a vital organ.* **2.** Necessary to life: *The heart and lungs are vital organs.* **3.** Very important; essential: *A good education is vital to a successful career.*

1. Your height and weight are **vital** statistics.

   part of speech _____ definition number _____

2. Clean water was a **vital** supply for the astronauts.

   part of speech _____ definition number _____

maul *noun* **1.** A heavy hammer, as one used for driving posts into the ground. Δ *verb* **1.** To injure by or as if by beating.

3. Our food tent had been **mauled** by the hungry bear.

   part of speech _____ definition number _____

4. Mrs. Jackson used a **maul** to split the wood for the campfire.

   part of speech _____ definition number _____

finish *verb* **1.** To bring or come to an end: *I have finished my lunch.* **2.** To use up. ∆ *noun* **1.** The conclusion; end: *The finish of the relay race was very close.* **2.** The final treatment or coating of a surface: *The finish on the table top was smooth and shiny.*

5. At the **finish** of the swim meet, our school had won the most races.

   part of speech _____ definition number _____

6. The painter used a clear **finish** to protect the wood from rotting.

   part of speech _____ definition number _____

7. There was barely enough time for Ling to **finish** her dinner before she had to rush off to choir practice.

   part of speech _____ definition number _____

E **TEST-TAKING STRATEGIES** **Analogies** help you to use critical thinking skills. They also appear on many tests, so practicing them will make you a better test taker.

Strategy: The key to solving analogies is figuring out how the words are related. Three kinds of relationships are explained below.

- one word is a kind, or type, of another word *(cat is a kind of vertebrate)*
- one word is a synonym for another word *(acute is a synonym for sensitive)*
- one word is an antonym of another word *(spotless is an antonym of filthy)*

Directions: Write the word that completes each analogy on the line.

1. Hawk is to predator as chair is to _____ .
   (table/furniture)

2. Carriage is to vehicle as soccer is to _____ . *(sport/cleat)*

3. Wrong is to mistaken as appointed is to _____ .
   (assigned/elected)

4. Olfactory is to nose as auditory is to _____ . *(mouth/ear)*

5. Immortal is to mortal as addition is to _____ .
   (math/subtraction)

G **TEST-TAKING STRATEGIES** On a **multiple-choice** test you are asked to choose an answer by filling in a "bubble." This exercise will give you practice with bubble answers.

Strategy: Read through the sentence and the answer choices. If there are choices that you are sure are *not* correct, skip those and focus on the remaining answers. When you select your answer, read the whole sentence through with your answer choice to make sure it is correct.

Directions: Fill in the bubble next to the word that best completes each sentence.

1. Rasheed learned to be a blacksmith by becoming a(n) _____ .

   Ⓐ election   Ⓑ apprentice   Ⓒ immortal   Ⓓ vertebrate

2. The Greek _____ about Atlas carrying the world on his back is one of my favorites.

   Ⓐ myth   Ⓑ realm   Ⓒ response   Ⓓ representative

3. *Charlotte's Web* is a(n) _____ tale about friendship and the circle of life.

   Ⓐ elected   Ⓑ tactile   Ⓒ timeless   Ⓓ appointed

4. Becoming class president seemed to be Delia's _____ .

   Ⓐ predator   Ⓑ species   Ⓒ carriage   Ⓓ fate

5. Many _____ of tree frog are found in the rain forests of South America.

   Ⓐ responses   Ⓑ vertebrates   Ⓒ species   Ⓓ psyches

ENRICHMENT WORDS

Draw a line between each Enrichment Word and its definition.

1.	deity	to assemble together
2.	proclamation	not active
3.	dormant	god or goddess
4.	nutritious	powerful or godlike
5.	convene	having substances for good health
6.	Olympian	public announcement

FORMING NEW WORDS

Skill Lesson
prefixes and suffixes

In the next set of lessons, you will learn how to break apart words to find the meaning. You will also learn how to put word parts together to form new words. The key to this is understanding parts of words.

A **PREFIXES AND SUFFIXES** You have already learned about suffixes. A **suffix** is a group of letters attached to a root at the end. For example, in the word *slowly*, the root is *slow* and the suffix is *-ly*. When a suffix is written alone, it often has a line before it to show where the rest of the word attaches. Suffixes often change the number, tense, or the part of speech of a word.

Each of the words below has a suffix. Decide what the suffix is and write it after the word. The first one is done for you.

1. goodness _____-ness_____

2. opening _____

3. commented _____

4. hopeful _____

5. endless _____

Another word part is called a **prefix.** This is a group of letters attached to the beginning of a word, before a root. At times, a prefix can also be just the first letters in a word. A prefix can give you important clues about the meaning of a word. Lessons 17, 18, and 19 will teach you important prefixes you can use in reading and writing. A prefix (like *sub-*) has a line after it to show where the root attaches.

One prefix you will learn is **sub-.** *Sub-* means "under" or "below." So when you come upon the word *subsoil* in your reading, you will know that it means "below the soil."

Another useful prefix to know is **super-,** which means "above," "over," or "very." Now that you know this, it is easy to figure out that a *superstructure* means a structure that is above or over another structure.

PREFIXES SUB- AND SUPER- Now see if you can use prefixes to determine the meaning of the boldfaced words in the following examples. Write the correct definition from the box to complete each sentence.

> *sub-* = below or under   *super-* = above, over, or very

1. The **subarea** of a building is _____ the main level.

2. A **supersharp** photograph is one that is _____ clear.

3. A **subcommittee** works _____ the main committee.

4. Your **superior** is someone who works _____ you.

5. A **subcrustal** lava flow is one that is _____ the earth's crust.

In the word *subarea* in example 1 above, it was easy to break down the meaning of the word by looking at its two parts: sub- + area = subarea. Sometimes a prefix is not attached to a whole word. In example 4, you can use the prefix *super-*, along with the sentence context and common sense, to help you figure out what *superior* means.

PREFIXES IN-, IL-, AND IM- There are other common and useful prefixes you can use to help you understand new words. One of these is *in-*, which means "not." It can also be spelled *il-* or *im-*. Here are some examples:

> **Inconsistent** means not all the same, or not consistent.
>
> **Illegible** means not clear, or not legible.
>
> **Impolite** means rude, or not polite.

Write a definition for each boldfaced word.

1. **Inactive** means _____ .

2. **Inappropriate** means _____ .

3. **Impractical** means _____ .

4. **Immeasurable** means _____ .

5. **Improbable** means _____ .

improbable

D **PREFIXES UNI-, BI-, AND TRI-** The prefixes *uni-*, *bi-*, and *tri-* are also useful to know. *Uni-* means "one," *bi-* means "two," and *tri-* means "three." Here are some examples:

A **unicycle** is a bike with <u>one</u> wheel.

A **biweekly** magazine comes out every <u>two</u> weeks.

A **triangle** has <u>three</u> angles.

Complete these examples that use the prefixes *uni-*, *bi-*, and *tri-*. Fill in the blank with the words *one*, *two*, or *three*.

1. A **triathlon** is a sporting event in which the athletes compete in

   _____ different races.

2. A **unitard** is a leotard-and-tights set that is all _____

   piece.

3. A **trimaran** is a sailboat with _____ hulls side by side.

4. To **unify** is to bring together many pieces into _____

   unit or whole.

5. Someone who is **bilingual** can speak _____ languages.

6. **Bifocals** are glasses that have _____ -part lenses.

7. A **unicorn** is a mythical beast with _____ horn.

8. A **tripod** is a support with _____ legs.

9. When you **bisect** something, you break or cut it into

   _____ parts.

tripod

unicycle

USING PREFIXES The following sentences contain words in boldfaced type that you will be learning in the next few lessons. See if you can figure out what the boldfaced words mean just by looking at the prefixes and the roots. Use the words in the box to help you fill in the blanks.

sub- = under or below	*super-* = above, over, or very
in-, il-, im- = not	*uni-* = one
bi- = two	*tri-* = three

1. **Subterranean** means _____ the ground.

2. **Bicentennial** means occurring every _____ hundred years.

3. **Immovable** means something is _____ movable.

4. **Intolerable** means _____ tolerable.

5. A **submarine** is a ship that floats _____ the water.

6. **Superheated** means _____ hot.

7. A **trilogy** is a set of _____ books, plays, or movies that go together.

8. **Unicellular** means having _____ cell.

9. **Illegal** means _____ legal.

10. **Subzero** means _____ zero.

11. **Improper** means _____ proper.

12. **Unique** means that it is _____ of a kind.

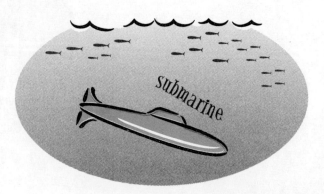

LESSON 17

Under and Over
prefixes sub- and super-

A You will find the prefixes *sub-* and *super-* useful in your general reading and writing, and in studying science. The prefix *sub-* means "under" or "below"; the prefix *super-* means "above," "very," or "over." This lesson presents words with *sub-* and *super-*.

1. **submarine** (sŭb' mə rēn')
   A **submarine** *is a ship that can go under water.* (noun)
   In Jules Verne's novel *Twenty Thousand Leagues Under the Sea*, Captain Nemo explores the ocean in a **submarine.**

2. **submerged** (səb mûrjd') *Something that is* **submerged** *is entirely under water.* (adjective)
   Entire houses were **submerged** during a terrible flood last spring.

3. **subservient** (səb sûr' vē ənt) *To be* **subservient** *is to be under another person's control; to be required to obey someone's orders.* (adjective)
   In Greek mythology, humans are **subservient** to the gods.

4. **subterranean** (sub' tə rā' nē ən)
   Something **subterranean** *is beneath the ground or hidden and secret.* (adjective)
   Subterranean water in the Missouri Ozarks is home to two types of rare, blind, white crayfish.

5. **subzero** (səb zîr' ō) **Subzero** *means below zero.* (adjective)
   We wore heavy coats walking in the **subzero** weather.

6. **superfluous** (soŏ pûr' floŏ əs)
   Something that is **superfluous** *is extra, or more than what is needed.* (adjective)
   The extra scoop of ice cream on my cone was **superfluous** because I already had more than I could eat.

7. **superheated** (soō' pər hē' tĭd)
   Something that is **superheated** *is very, very hot.* (adjective)
   The volcano sent lava and **superheated** ash rolling down into villages.

8. **superimposed** (soō' pər ĭm pozd')
   Something that is **superimposed** *has been placed over something else.* (adjective)
   Some special effects are made when computer-created images are **superimposed** on a real background.

Draw a line between each vocabulary word and its definition.

1. subzero   below zero
2. subservient   overheated
3. superheated   underground
4. subterranean   under orders

All the boldfaced words in the passage below include the prefixes *sub-* or *super-*. Read the passage. Then do the exercises that follow.

Bacteria Are Everywhere!

What can live in **subzero** ice packs, **submerged** in boiling water, and even without air? Why bacteria, of course! Although we often think of these one-celled life forms as agents of disease, bacteria can also help us.

We can thank bacteria for milk. One type lives in the largest of the cow's four stomachs. It takes the tough cover of grass, called *cellulose*, and changes it into food that the cow makes into milk. Other bacteria can then change the milk to yogurt.

Bacteria take elements in the air, such as carbon and nitrogen, and change them into forms that can be digested by living things. Far from being **superfluous**, bacteria are necessary to all life forms.

While some bacteria live on land, others inhabit the deepest **subterranean** recesses of the ocean, far beneath the ocean floor. Exploring with the aid of **submarines,** scientists have found bacteria in **superheated** vents that extend from the earth's center out to the ocean floor. These bacteria create food from the chemicals in the water.

Recently, explorers drilling for oil have found bacteria more than 1,500 feet under the ocean floor. They live under intense pressure, with no air. They survive on methane gas that is up to four million years old.

By taking advantage of their strange appetites, scientists have learned to use bacteria to clean up oil spills. Bacteria can be made **subservient** in this task by first feeding a diet of oil to a large sample of bacteria. Then, after a big oil spill, a layer of bacteria is **superimposed** on the mess, and the bacteria eat the oil. The digested oil becomes harmless carbon dioxide and water.

WORD LIST

submarine

submerged

subservient

subterranean

subzero

superfluous

superheated

superimposed

1. What is one way that bacteria are helpful to humans?

_____

_____

2. What are two places bacteria can live? What words tell you this?

_____

_____

C Break apart each word into its **prefix** and **root.** Write the prefix and root on the line, as shown in the example.

1. subservient = ____sub- + servient____

2. subzero = _____

3. superheat = _____

4. submarine = _____

5. superimpose = _____

D Choose the vocabulary word that best describes the situation in each sentence. Write the word on the line.

1. Heat a liquid to the boiling point without changing it into vapor.

_____ *(submarine/superheat/superimpose)*

2. Place the image of the rainbow on top of the picture of the blue sky.

_____ *(superfluous/subservient/superimpose)*

3. The cave, deep in the earth, was dark, damp, and cool.

_____ *(submarine/submerge/subterranean)*

4. One kind of ship can work both on the water and beneath the water.

_____ *(submarine/subservient/subzero)*

5. Renting both a movie and a video game for the evening was too much.

_____ *(subservient/superfluous/subterranean)*

Name

Date

E Complete each sentence with a phrase that makes sense. Note that another form of a vocabulary word has been used.

1. Crew members on a **submarine** should expect _____

_____ .

2. If you make a **subterranean** exploration, you go _____

_____ .

3. In **subzero** weather, you should wear _____

_____ .

4. To **submerge** something, _____

_____ .

5. A **subservient** person _____

_____ .

ENRICHMENT WORDS

Here are two more words that use the prefixes *super-* and *sub-*.
Try to figure out what they mean before you read the definitions.

1. **superabundant** (soo' pər ə **bun'** dant) **Superabundant** *means more than usual, too much.* (adjective)
My puppy's **superabundant** energy tires me out.

2. **subculture** (sub' kŭl' chər) *A* **subculture** *is one part of a culture.* (noun)
There are many different Native American **subcultures.**

OFF THE PAGE

Create a picture of **super-** and **sub-** words. Divide a piece of paper into a top half and a bottom half. Label the top half "Super Words." Label the bottom half "Sub Words." Write the vocabulary words in the proper half. Then think of other **sub-** and **super-** words to add. Draw pictures to help show the meanings of some of the words.

LESSON 18

"Not" Again!
prefixes in-, il-, im-

A Because it means "not," the prefix *in-* changes a word into an opposite. For example, *indirect* means "not direct." This prefix can be a bit tricky because it can be spelled three ways: *in-*, *il-*, and *im-*.

1. **illegal** (ĭ lē' gəl) *Something* **illegal** *is not lawful.* (adjective)
It is **illegal** for cars to pass a stop sign without stopping first.

2. **illogical** (ĭ lŏj' ĭ kəl) *Something that is* **illogical** *does not make sense.* (adjective)
It's **illogical** to think that the world is flat after pictures from the moon have shown it to be round.

3. **immodest** (ĭ mŏd' ĭst) *To be* **immodest** *is to show off; to be boastful.* (adjective)
The **immodest** boy boasted about his good grades to his friends.

4. **immovable** (ĭ mōō' və bəl) *Something that is* **immovable** *cannot be moved or changed.* (adjective)
The huge rock was **immovable**.

5. **immune** (ĭ myōōn') *To be* **immune** *from something is to be not affected by it or resistant to it.* (adjective)
After you get chicken pox, you usually become **immune** to the disease and won't get it again.

6. **imperfection** (ĭm' pər fĕk' shən) *An* **imperfection** *is a flaw, or defect, that makes something not perfect.* (noun)
A diamond with an **imperfection** is worth less than a perfect diamond.

7. **improper** (ĭm prŏp' ər) *Something* **improper** *is not suitable.* (adjective)
It is **improper** to eat steak with your fingers.

8. **intolerable** (ĭn tŏl' ər ə bəl) *Something* **intolerable** *cannot be tolerated; it is unbearable.* (adjective)
Lee found the violence in the video **intolerable,** so he turned it off.

Draw a line between each vocabulary word and its definition.

1. illegal	resistant
2. immune	flaw
3. intolerable	not bearable
4. imperfection	not lawful
5. improper	lacking modesty
6. immodest	not suitable

The boldfaced words in the passage below all contain prefixes meaning "not." Read the passage. Then answer the questions that follow.

Clothing in the Middle Ages

Do you have family members who constantly point out **imperfections** in your clothing? Have you ever been asked to leave a store because you weren't wearing shoes? If you find such things annoying, be glad you are not living in the Middle Ages, when there were laws about what kind of clothing people could wear.

In the Middle Ages, people were expected to dress according to their social class. People in power tried to keep the class system **immovable** by passing "Sumptuary Laws," which described proper and **improper** dress. It was particularly **intolerable** for middle- or lower-class people to wear expensive clothes or jewelry. This was considered most **immodest.**

In Bologna, Italy, the wearing of jewels, belts, embroidery, fur, dresses, and shoes was strictly limited. Laws were passed to specify the number of buttons that could be worn.

In England in the 1500s, it was **illegal** for everyone except kings and nobles to wear purple. Crimson, scarlet, and blue velvet could be worn by any noble, but not by commoners. These laws seem **illogical** to us today, but there may have been some practical purpose for them. For example, dyes were expensive. Of course, the queen stood above the laws and could, at any time, make her friends **immune** from them. Then they could wear as much red or purple as they wanted.

WORD LIST

illegal

illogical

immodest

immovable

immune

imperfection

improper

intolerable

1. What are some of the laws about clothing in the Middle Ages?

_____

_____

2. Why do the laws from the 1500s seem illogical to us today? Use at least two of the boldfaced words to explain.

_____

_____

C Choose the word that best completes each sentence. Write it on the line.

1. The sweater was on sale because there was an _____ in the fabric. (*illegal/improper/imperfection*)

2. It is _____ to drive without a license. (*immovable/illogical/illegal*)

3. Vaccinations can make people _____ to certain diseases, such as smallpox. (*immune/improper/immodest*)

4. It is considered _____ to talk loudly in the library. (*imperfection/improper/illegal*)

5. The wall of sandbags was an _____ barrier that held back the raging river. (*intolerable/immovable/illogical*)

D Write a synonym from the word list for each pair of words.

1. nonsense, silly _____

2. unlawful, prohibited _____

3. flaw, mistake _____

4. stuck, unchangeable _____

5. boasting, bragging _____

OTHER FORMS

illegally
illogically
immodestly
immunization
immunity
imperfect
improperly
intolerably
intolerant

E Complete each sentence with a phrase that fits. Note that some other forms of the vocabulary words are used in the sentences.

1. If someone is **illegally** parked, _____

   _____ .

2. An example of an **immovable** object is _____

   _____ .

3. Something I consider **intolerably** boring is _____

   _____ .

4. An example of **improper** dress at a formal gathering would be

   _____ .

5. An example of an **immodest** remark is _____

   _____ .

ENRICHMENT WORDS

Here are two more words that have a prefix that means "not." Can you figure out their meanings without reading the definitions?

1. **impersonal** (ĭm pûr' sən əl) *Something that is* **impersonal** *shows no emotion or personality.* (adjective)

   The **impersonal** greeting read, "To whom it may concern."

2. **invariably** (ĭn vâr' ē ə blē) **Invariably** *means always.* (adverb)

   People **invariably** close their eyes when they sneeze.

OFF THE PAGE

Choose a vocabulary word. Then write a paragraph that compares the word with its base form. For example, you could compare **improper** dress at your school with proper dress. Or, you could compare something **illegal** with something legal.

LESSON 19

One, Two, Three...
prefixes uni-, bi-, tri-

a biped

A Some prefixes give hints about word meanings by telling us about numbers. This lesson deals with common number prefixes. *Uni-* means "one," *bi-* means "two," and *tri-* means "three."

1. **unicellular** (yoo nĭ **sĕl'** yə lər) *A* **unicellular** *living thing has only one cell.* (adjective)
The amoeba is a **unicellular** organism.

2. **unique** (yoo **nēk'**) *If something is* **unique** *there is nothing else like it; it is special.* (adjective)
Of all animals, human beings are **unique** in their language abilities.

3. **universe** (**yoo'** nə vûrs') *The* **universe** *consists of everything that exists, including stars and planets.* (noun)
Our **universe** contains the Milky Way, which has billions of stars.

4. **bicentennial** (bī' sĕn **tĕn'** ē əl) *A* **bicentennial** *is the two-hundredth anniversary of an event.* (noun)
Ohio was admitted to the United States in 1803, so it celebrates its **bicentennial** in 2003.

5. **biped** (**bī'** pĕd') *A* **biped** *is an animal that walks on two feet.* (noun)
A bird is a **biped**.

6. **trilogy** (**trĭl'** ə jē) *A* **trilogy** *is a set of three books, plays, films, or stories that are related in subject or theme.* (noun)
What were the names of the three movies in the famous space film **trilogy?**

7. **triple** (**trĭp'** əl) *Something that is* **triple** *is three times as many; made up of three parts.* (adjective)
The champion ice skater could do **triple** axels, turning three times in the air.

8. **trivial** (**trĭv'** ē əl) *Something* **trivial** *is not important.* (adjective)
In ancient Rome people met to gossip, or talk about unimportant things, at a place where three roads met, so *tri* ("three") + *via* ("road") = **trivial.**

Draw a line between each vocabulary word and its definition.

1. biped   total existence
2. universe   one of a kind
3. unique   three times
4. triple   two-footed

© Great Source DO NOT COPY

The boldfaced words in the passage below all tell something about numbers. Read the passage. Then answer the questions that follow.

Dinosaurs—Gone, But Not Forgotten

Sixty-six million years ago, dinosaurs were kings of the earth. Although this **unique** animal species is gone, dinosaurs still fascinate us. One famous movie **trilogy** is based on the idea of a scientist who brings dinosaurs back to roam the world.

Some dinosaurs were huge. At about 50 feet tall, the Brachiosaurus was more than **triple** the height of a giraffe. Dinosaurs such as Tyrannosaurus rex, Gigantosaurus, and Carcharodontosaurus were the largest meat-eating animals that ever lived. One weighed almost two thousand pounds. But other dinosaurs were small. The Unenlagia was only four feet tall. Like a bird, it was a **biped** with hollow bones, but it probably could not fly.

Why did dinosaurs disappear? They didn't all die out at once. Different types of dinosaurs became extinct at different times. But all the dinosaurs that were alive 65 million years ago, as well as many other creatures, suddenly vanished. Many reasons have been put forth. One theory that is gaining popularity is that a huge asteroid traveling through our **universe** may have hit the earth. The effects of such an impact would not be **trivial.** It would have caused darkness and cold, acid rain, and huge forest fires, burning the dinosaurs, as well as many other species living on earth at that time. Although the largest life forms died out, the smallest, **unicellular** life forms were able to survive, perhaps underground.

The asteroid theory is supported by findings of iridium, a chemical common in outer space, and of soot, possibly from an explosion. In 1990, scientists looking for the depression that such a huge asteroid would create found one in Mexico, on the Yucatan Peninsula. Questions still remain, though—for example, Where did the asteroid come from?

The year 2018 will be the **bicentennial** of Solomon Ellsworth's important discovery of dinosaur bones. People were fascinated by these huge and mysterious bones. Two hundred years later, dinosaur bones and dinosaur mysteries continue to fascinate us.

WORD LIST

unicellular

unique

universe

bicentennial

biped

trilogy

triple

trivial

1. Use one of the boldfaced words to describe something we know about dinosaurs. _____

_____

2. If Brachiosaurus was more than triple the height of a giraffe, about how tall is a giraffe? _____

_____

C Replace the underlined word or phrase with a word from the list that has the same meaning.

1. Don't waste your time on <u>unimportant</u>, or _____, pursuits.

2. A <u>one-celled</u>, or _____, organism is so small that it can only be seen through a microscope.

3. J.R.R. Tolkein wrote a popular <u>set of three books</u>, or _____, called *The Lord of the Rings*.

4. I've made a <u>one-of-a-kind</u>, or _____, necklace for my mother.

5. A big parade was planned to celebrate the town's <u>two-hundredth anniversary</u>, or _____ .

D List the words from the list above in the boxes in which they fit best. Then go back and add at least one more word using *tri-*, *bi-*, and *uni-* in each box.

Three	Two	One
_____	_____	_____
_____	_____	_____
_____	_____	_____
_____	_____	_____

E Complete each sentence with a phrase that makes sense. Note that some other forms of the vocabulary words are used in the sentences.

1. A **biped** has _____

_____ .

2. If you **triple** your $5 allowance, you will have _____

_____ .

3. If you are **uniquely** qualifed to do something, _____

_____ .

4. If a person is **universally** admired, _____

_____ .

5. A **trilogy** has _____

_____ .

ENRICHMENT WORDS

Here are two more words that use a prefix that tells about number. If a bilingual person speaks two languages, how many languages would a trilingual person speak?

1. **bilingual** (bī lĭng' gwəl) *A* **bilingual** *person speaks two languages.* (adjective)

   Bernadette is **bilingual** in Tagalog and English.

2. **triathlon** (trī ăth' lən) *A* **triathlon** *is a long-distance race with three parts: running, swimming, and bicycling.* (noun)

   A person has to train for years to be ready to compete in a **triathlon.**

triathlon

OFF THE PAGE

Choose one of these topics to write about in a paragraph.

1. Describe a **triple** play in baseball.

2. What are three **trivial** ways to spend your time? For example, you might spend your time linking paper clips together in a chain.

LESSON 20

Review
lessons 16-19

In this lesson, you will review the words and skills you have learned in the last four lessons. This will help you to remember them.

A **MATCHING WORDS AND DEFINITIONS**
Write the word from the box that matches each definition.

> subservient   immune   superfluous   improper   trivial   trilogy

1. required to obey someone else _____

2. resistant to or unaffected by _____

3. not suitable _____

4. more than is needed _____

5. unimportant _____

6. a series of three _____

B **USING WORDS IN CONTEXT** Use the words in the box to complete the paragraph.

> submerged   intolerable   unique   immodest   universe   subzero

The life of an explorer is a (1) _____ one, for nothing is like it. I hope I am not being (2) _____ when I say that I think I would make an excellent explorer. You see, I enjoy being in situations that others might find (3) _____ because they are so uncomfortable or even dangerous. One adventure might find me exploring sea life, (4) _____ far below the surface of the ocean. Next, I might end up in the arctic, enduring (5) _____ temperatures as well as complete isolation. As space travel becomes more common, I may be able to explore the far reaches of the (6) _____. Finally, I would settle down to write a book and let others know about the fun I had!

WRITING WORDS IN SENTENCES Choose two of the words on each line to use in a sentence. You can change the form of the word if you like. (For example, *submerged* may be changed to *submerge*.)

1. submerged   subterranean   superheated

   _____

   _____

2. submarine   imperfection   triple

   _____

   _____

3. bicentennial   improper   immodest

   _____

   _____

4. illegal   trivial   unique

   _____

   _____

D **PREFIXES** Read the sentences below and determine the meaning from the **prefix** and the **context** of the sentence. Circle the letter of the word or phrase that best defines the word in boldface type.

1. Our firm's **biannual** meeting was a big success.

   A. occurring every year

   B. occurring every hundred years

   C. occurring twice a year

2. The scribbled letter was **illegible**.

   A. well-written

   B. clean

   C. not readable

3. An avalanche had made the ravine **impassable.**

   A. not scenic

   B. not able to be passed through

   C. worn and smooth

4. Gathering her courage, Rachel asked her **supervisor** for a raise.

   A. person who oversees another's work

   B. person who works for you

   C. person who works for another company

5. All the students answered the teacher in **unison.**

   A. immediately

   B. over again

   C. at one time

E **TEST-TAKING STRATEGIES** An **analogy** compares word pairs that are related in some way. An analogy can be expressed in a sentence or with colons (the single colon means "is to" and the double colon means "as").

> *Superfluous* is to *extra* as *illegal* is to *unlawful.*
> Superfluous : extra :: illegal : unlawful

Strategy: To solve the analogies below, practice reading each one to yourself as a whole sentence, using the words "is to" and "as" in place of the colons.

Directions: Write the word that completes each analogy.

1. pleasant : intolerable : : immovable : _____ *flexible/solid*

2. superimpose : overlap : : imperfect : _____
   excellent/flawed

3. submarine : submerge : : universe : _____
   triple/unicellular

4. subzero : temperature : : illogical : _____ *warmth/answer*

5. lion : vertebrate : : bird : _____ *robin/biped*

F **TEST-TAKING STRATEGIES** On a **multiple-choice** test you are asked to choose an answer by filling in a "bubble."

Strategy: Read through the words and the answer choices. If there are choices that you are sure are *not* correct, skip those and focus on the remaining answers.

Directions: Fill in the bubble next to the word that gives the meaning of the underlined prefix.

1. <u>uni</u>cellular   <u>uni</u>verse
   (A) not   (C) one
   (B) under   (D) over

2. <u>im</u>mune   <u>im</u>perfection
   (A) above   (C) one
   (B) three   (D) not

3. <u>il</u>legal   <u>il</u>logical
   (A) one   (C) over
   (B) not   (D) under

4. <u>bi</u>centennial   <u>bi</u>ped
   (A) one   (C) three
   (B) two   (D) not

5. <u>sub</u>terranean   <u>sub</u>servient
   (A) under   (C) not
   (B) over   (D) two

6. <u>super</u>impose   <u>super</u>fluous
   (A) very   (C) three
   (B) under   (D) over

ENRICHMENT WORDS

Draw a line between each Enrichment Word and its definition.

1. superabundant   speaking two languages
2. subculture   showing no emotion
3. impersonal   three-part long-distance race
4. invariably   more than enough
5. bilingual   always
6. triathlon   part of a culture

GOING BEYOND WORDS

Skill Lesson
using a thesaurus

The English language is rich in words that mean the same—or about the same—as other words. We have already learned that words that have the same meaning are called **synonyms.** For example, *big* and *large* are synonyms. A good place to find synonyms is in a **thesaurus.**

USING THE THESAURUS When you find yourself using the same word too many times, make your writing more interesting by looking in a thesaurus to find other ways to say the same thing. Let's look at an example. Circle the word *big* each time it occurs.

> At the center of the circus was a big tent. All around it were big and small booths with games to play or trinkets to buy. Inside was a big circle where the animals and people performed. There was a dancing bear and some trick bicycle riders. Tim's favorite was a big elephant who stood on its hind legs and answered questions by nodding its head yes or no.

As a writer, you should vary your word choice. To do that, use a thesaurus. Here is the thesaurus entry for *big:*

> **big** *adjective* **1.** colossal, enormous, gigantic, huge, immense, large **2.** important, great, major, significant, vital

The thesaurus entry for *big* offers several words to choose from. But how do you choose? Many of the words a thesaurus gives mean about the same thing, but they differ slightly. These slight differences are called **shades of meaning.** You will learn some words with different shades of meaning in Lesson 22.

Notice that in the thesaurus entry for *big,* the words listed under 1 mean "big in size" and the words listed under 2 mean "big in importance." All the words mean *big,* but in slightly different ways.

Now let's improve the paragraph about the circus. Choose one of the words from the thesaurus entry for *big* to fill in each blank below. Think about whether you will choose from list 1 or list 2. Use a dictionary if you are not sure of the different shades of meaning.

At the center of the circus was a **(1)** _____ tent. All around it were **(2)** _____ and small booths with games to play or trinkets to buy. Inside was a **(3)** _____ circle where the animals and people performed. There was a dancing bear and some trick bicycle riders. The trick bicycle riders were a

(4) _____ attraction. Tim's favorite was a

(5) _____ elephant who stood on its hind legs.

B **SHADES OF MEANING** Here are some more examples of words that have different shades of meaning. Read each pair of words and write the one that best completes each sentence. Use a dictionary if you need help understanding the shades of meaning.

small   tiny

1. The _____ insect could hardly be seen.

2. Jared hiked through the thick woods to a _____ meadow.

bad   terrible

3. The sinking of the *Titanic* was a _____ tragedy.

4. The chilly temperature and still air made it a _____ day for kite flying.

hill   mountain

5. David and Mercedes had an easy hike up the _____ .

6. The huge _____ was like a wall between the two cities.

looked   peeked

7. The detective _____ at the clues for a long time before solving the case.

8. Janine quickly _____ inside the mysterious box when she thought no one was watching.

USING A DICTIONARY Now try these examples. Dictionary entries for two words appear above each pair of sentences. Think about the shade of meaning that the context of the sentence calls for. Then write the correct word to complete each sentence.

de-light-ful (dĭ līt' fŭl) Greatly pleasing. *adjective*

good (gŏŏd) Having positive or desirable qualities; not bad or poor. *adjective*

1. Although it was old, the barn was still useable and in

   _____ repair.

2. Meeting his favorite actor had been a _____ surprise for Wyatt.

probe (prōb) To investigate or explore. *verb*

ask (ăsk) To put a question to. *verb*

3. Anisa did not want to _____ Hareem any more questions about the homework.

4. The commission decided to _____ into the cause of the accident.

meal (mēl) The food served and eaten in one sitting. *noun*

feast (fēst) A large elaborate meal, especially one prepared for a special occasion; a banquet. *noun*

5. This _____ was just like any other, as far as Sadie was concerned.

6. A large _____ was prepared in honor of the royal wedding.

feast

noise (noiz) Sound. *noun*

rack-et (răk' ĭt) A loud, unpleasant noise; uproar. *noun*

7. The only _____ they could hear was the low-level hum

   coming from the machinery.

8. "Now cut out that _____ !" Gina hollered at her

   brother.

an-gry (ăng' grē) Feeling or showing displeasure or hostility. *adjective*

fu-ri-ous (fyo͝or' ē əs) Full of or marked by extreme anger; raging.
adjective

9. Stefan was so _____ when he learned he had not made

   the team that he ran out of the gym, slamming the door behind him.

10. Keshia was more hurt than _____ when she found out

    she had not been chosen to represent her class at the science fair.

avoid (ə void') To keep away from; stay clear of. *verb*

shun (shŭn) To avoid deliberately and consistently. *verb*

11. Trying to _____ looking in her eyes, Colby lied about

    the broken vase to his mother.

12. I am a loner and therefore _____ asking for help with

    anything.

D **REVISING A PARAGRAPH** Use the thesaurus entry
below to revise the paragraph. Fill in each blank with an appro-
priate word for *darkness*.

darkness *noun* **1.** dimness, murk, blackness, gloom, gloominess
2. dusk, evening, night, nightfall, nighttime

It was getting late. **Darkness** was everywhere. As the **darkness** fell,
Julian could feel the **darkness** seep into his bones. **Darkness** would soon
take over.

It was getting late. **(1)** _____ was everywhere. As the

(2) _____ fell, Julian could feel the **(3)** _____

seep into his bones. **(4)** _____ would soon take over.

Good or Bad?
shades of meaning

youthful

A Are you good at picking up hints? Some words hint at good or bad meanings. Such words are said to have *connotations*. All of the words below have good (positive) or bad (negative) connotations. As you study these words, think about the shades of meaning that were introduced to you in Lesson 21.

1. **observant** (əb zûr' vənt) *An* **observant** *person carefully notices things.* (adjective)
Cheryl was so **observant** that she saw every tiny change in the ant farm.

2. **prying** (prī' ĭng) *A* **prying** *person snoops into things that should be private.* (adjective)
The famous singer protects her family from **prying** reporters.

3. **youthful** (yōoth' fəl) *A* **youthful** *person is young and energetic.* (adjective)
My **youthful** grandmother often goes in-line skating with me.

4. **immature** (ĭm' ə tyŏor') *An* **immature** *person is childish and self-centered.* (adjective)
My **immature** ten-year-old brother kicked the furniture in anger when he was not allowed to watch a movie.

5. **fearless** (fîr' lĭs) *A* **fearless** *person is brave and does not feel fear.* (adjective)
George Washington was a **fearless** soldier who often led his men into battle.

6. **reckless** (rĕk' lĭs) *A* **reckless** *person is careless and takes stupid or silly risks.* (adjective)
Two **reckless** drivers raced on a crowded highway.

7. **determined** (dĭ tûr' mĭnd) *Someone who is* **determined** *is serious and dedicated to achieving a goal.* (adjective)
Mariah was **determined** to get an *A* on her science project.

8. **stubborn** (stŭb' ərn) *A* **stubborn** *person is not willing to give in or change.* (adjective)
Jim isn't a good team member because he is so **stubborn** that he always wants to do things his way.

Draw a line between each vocabulary word and its definition.

1. youthful   careless
2. determined   young and energetic
3. reckless   dedicated
4. immature   childish
5. stubborn   brave
6. fearless   unwilling to change

All the boldfaced words in the passage below have either positive or negative connotations. Read the passage. Then answer the questions that follow.

Dr. Sally Ride: Tennis Player, Astronaut, Professor

Dr. Sally Ride was the first American woman astronaut, but that was just one of her three career possibilities. One of her **youthful** interests was tennis. She played so well that tennis star Billy Jean King told her to become a professional. Instead, she decided to study physics at Stanford University. Sally was an excellent student, and was on her way to becoming a professor—until she learned that NASA was looking for astronauts.

NASA wanted intelligent astronauts who could also handle physical tasks. Another requirement was good judgment and the ability to follow orders. **Immature** or **stubborn** people can be dangerous on a space mission. NASA screened carefully, even asking questions that might be considered **prying,** but that were important in a life and death situation. In the end, Sally Ride was one of 35 people chosen out of more than 8,000 applicants.

Determined to excel, Ride trained in parachute jumping, water survival, and weightlessness. She was a **fearless** flyer who enjoyed being a pilot so much that it soon became her hobby. Ride became a radio communications specialist for the space mission. She had to be **observant** in monitoring her equipment so that nothing could go wrong, for communication with earth was critical to space missions. But Sally did other things too. She even helped design a remote mechanical arm.

Sally Ride went into space twice, and was preparing to go again when the *Challenger* space craft exploded. Shocked, the public demanded an explanation to see if any **reckless** act had caused the accident. Ride was appointed by the president to help investigate the disaster. Later she worked in NASA's Office of Exploration.

Dr. Ride has now retired from NASA and is a professor at Stanford University. One of her goals is to help young girls become interested in science and mathematics.

WORD LIST

determined

fearless

immature

observant

prying

reckless

stubborn

youthful

1. Which of Sally Ride's youthful accomplishments hinted that she would succeed as an astronaut? Why do you think so?

   _____

   _____

2. What words tell you about Sally Ride's qualities as an astronaut?

   _____

   _____

C List the words from the word list in the boxes in which they fit best.

Good Connotations	Bad Connotations

D Choose the right word to fit into each sentence. Write the word on the line.

1. I try not to ask _____ questions about other people's personal lives. (*observant/prying*)

2. Molly is so _____ that she won't listen to reason. (*stubborn/determined*)

3. If I were going to learn rock climbing, I'd want a _____ instructor. (*reckless/fearless*)

4. Miguel's _____ enthusiasm about dinosaurs was refreshing to the professor. (*immature/youthful*)

5. It's _____ to try to feed bears in the wild. (*reckless/fearless*)

OTHER FORMS

determination

fearlessly

immaturely

observe

pry

recklessness

stubbornly

youthfulness

E Complete each sentence with a phrase that makes sense. Note that some other forms of the vocabulary words are used.

1. I marched **fearlessly** into _____

   _____ .

2. It is important to be **observant** when _____

   _____ .

3. When someone behaves **immaturely,** _____

   _____ .

4. It's not nice to **pry** because _____

   _____ .

5. If you are **determined** to do something, _____

   _____ .

ENRICHMENT WORDS

Here are two more words that have good and bad meanings. Which is the "good" word?

1. **scholar** (skŏl' ər) *A* **scholar** *is a learned person who has studied hard and gained a great deal of knowledge.* (noun)

   The **scholar** of ancient languages was called in to read the newly discovered Hieroglyphic scroll.

2. **drudge** (drŭj) *A* **drudge** *is one who works hard at doing boring and unpleasant work.* (noun)

   If you don't enjoy the work you are doing, you will feel like a **drudge** at the end of the day.

OFF THE PAGE

Choose one of the word pairs from this lesson, for example, **determined** and **stubborn.** Use examples from books, movies, and real life that show how the connotation is different for each word. For example,

Cinderella was determined to go to the ball.

Cinderella's step-sisters stubbornly refused to let her go.

determined

It's All Greek
words from ancient Greeks

A The ancient Greeks who lived more than 2,500 years ago had an important and advanced culture. The city of Athens was a center of learning, and Sparta was known for its attention to athletics. Many ancient Greek words are still used today.

1. **academic** (ăk' ə děm' ĭk) *Something* **academic** *refers to school subjects or knowledge.* (adjective)
In school we learn **academic** subjects, such as social studies and science, as well as other subjects, such as music and physical education.

2. **colossal** (kə lŏs' əl) *Something* **colossal** *is huge.* (adjective)
Colossal Mount Everest is the tallest peak on earth.

3. **Herculean** (hûr' ky lē' ən)
A **Herculean** *task requires great strength and effort.* (adjective)
With snow drifts piled up to twenty feet, plowing the sidewalks was a **Herculean** task.

4. **mentor** (měn' tôr') *A* **mentor** *is a wise, trusted advisor, counselor, or teacher.* (noun)
The basketball coach acted as a **mentor** to the girls on her team.

5. **Midas touch** (mī' dəs tŭch) *A person with a* **Midas touch** *makes money easily.* (noun phrase) People who have started Internet companies and made millions of dollars seem to have the **Midas touch.**

6. **odyssey** (ŏd' ĭ sē) *An* **odyssey** *is a long, adventurous journey.* (noun)
The long, dangerous boat trip was an **odyssey** of hope and courage.

7. **panic** (păn' ĭk) **Panic** *is a feeling of sudden and extreme fear.* (noun)
Her **panic** went away when she realized that she was being rescued from the stuck elevator.

8. **skeptical** (skěp' tĭk əl) *People who are* **skeptical** *are doubtful.* (adjective)
The teacher was **skeptical** when Taylor said the dog ate her homework.

Draw a line between each vocabulary word and its definition.

1. panic   doubtful
2. skeptical   long, adventurous trip
3. odyssey   feeling of fear
4. Herculean   requiring great strength
5. Midas touch   huge
6. academic   advisor
7. colossal   having to do with school subjects
8. mentor   creates wealth

B The boldfaced words in the passage below are about a very generous man named Albert Lexie. Read the passage. Then answer the questions that follow.

Albert Lexie: The Charitable Touch

It isn't hard to find Albert in the hospital—just ask for the shoeshine man. The **colossal** sums of money Albert Lexie has donated to sick children have made him famous in the Children's Hospital of Pittsburgh.

Albert Lexie's personal **odyssey** changed him from a person who needed help into a person who gives help. Born poor and developmentally disabled, he struggled hard in **academic** subjects. But, one day he saw some boys making shoeshine boxes in shop class. That's when he decided on his profession.

In 1979, Albert watched a telethon that was raising money for children's health care. Inspired, he decided that he would dedicate his life to this cause. Albert didn't have a **Midas touch;** in fact he earned less than ten thousand dollars that year. There was no **mentor** in Albert's life to show him how to raise money. But Albert had determination, and, through a **Herculean** effort, he raised more than seven hundred dollars to donate that year. A friend took him to visit the hospital he had helped, and the director offered him a job shining shoes for the staff.

All of Albert's tips go to help poor children who need medical services. Over the years, Lexie has donated over forty-four thousand dollars. His beloved mother has died, and he now lives in his own apartment. Although he may have been **skeptical** at first that he would be happy living alone, Albert now enjoys his independent life.

Albert is constantly in touch with others through his charity. He understands the **panic** a mother feels when she does not have enough money to help a sick child. Because of Albert Lexie's efforts, many of these children now receive medical care. Each month, he visits children in the hospital, and many have come to think of him as a role model.

WORD LIST

academic

colossal

Herculean

mentor

Midas touch

odyssey

panic

skeptical

1. Circle three boldfaced words in the passage that describe Albert Lexie. Then explain your choices on the lines below.

_____

_____

2. How does Albert's income and life style form a contrast to the money he gives to charity?

_____

_____

C Read about the history of the vocabulary words. Use the boldfaced clues to write the vocabulary word that fits. Then write what each word means now.

The Meaning Then	Vocabulary Word	The Meaning Now
1. **Odysseus** was a leader of the Greeks whose adventurous journey took ten years.		
2. **Mentor** was a trusted advisor to Odysseus.		
3. The **Colossus** of Rhodes was a statue so huge ships could pass between its legs.		
4. In Greek mythology, King **Midas** wished for everything he touched to turn to **gold.**		
5. The Greek philosopher Plato **taught** at the **Akadēmeia.**		
6. **Hercules** was a Greek hero who had to do twelve difficult tasks to become immortal.		
7. **Skeptics** believed that real knowledge was impossible.		
8. The god **Pan** (half human and half horse) produced a feeling of fear in humans.		

OTHER FORMS

academy

mentoring

panicky

skeptic

D Complete each sentence with a phrase that makes sense. Note that some other forms of the vocabulary words have been used.

1. If you had a **Midas touch,** _____
   _____ .

2. Sometimes people feel **panicky** when _____
   _____ .

3. My favorite **academic** subject is _____
   _____ .

4. I'm a real **skeptic** when it comes to stories about _____
   _____ .

5. I would like a **mentor** to help me learn _____
   _____ .

ENRICHMENT WORDS

Here are two more words that come from the Greek language. Try using these words in your conversation this week.

1. chaos (ka' os') **Chaos** *is a state of total disorder and confusion. Chaos comes from a Greek word that means "disorder of the universe."* (noun)

   A power failure left the city in **chaos.**

2. Spartan (spär' tn) **Spartan** *things are lacking in comfort or require self-discipline. The Greek city of Sparta was known for its training of athletes and warriors.* (adjective)

   The **Spartan** training program required soccer players to practice eight hours per day and get to bed by 7 P.M.

OFF THE PAGE

Something colossal is not just big, it's really, really big! Add three words of your own. It starts on the left with words that describe a small size and ends with the biggest of all—colossal—on the right.

Miniscule ⇨ tiny ⇨   ⇨   ⇨   ⇨ colossal

Great Advice

proverbs

A Has anyone ever said to you, "Birds of a feather flock together"? What a funny thing to say! In this case, the person means, "People who are alike enjoy being together." A proverb is a way of telling you a common truth. Which of these proverbs have you heard?

1. A **proverb** is a short, common, wise saying that gives advice or states a rule about life. (noun)

2. **Birds of a feather flock together** means that people with similar personalities or interests tend to spend time together.

3. **Don't judge a book by its cover** means don't judge people or things by their appearances.

4. **Great oaks from little acorns grow** means that large or great things often start out small.

5. **Look before you leap** means you should consider carefully what might happen before you do something.

6. **Never leave till tomorrow that which you can do today** means do things as soon as you can.

7. **Small strokes fell great oaks** means steady, small actions will eventually accomplish something big.

8. **A stitch in time saves nine** means that if you repair things as soon as possible, you can avoid having to fix a bigger problem later.

Draw a line between each proverb and its explanation.

1. Never leave till tomorrow that which you can do today.

    Think carefully.

2. Birds of a feather flock together.

    Do it now.

3. Great oaks from little acorns grow.

    Big things start out small.

4. Look before you leap.

    Like attracts like.

The boldfaced proverbs are explained in the passage below. Read the passage. Then answer the questions that follow.

Words of Wisdom

Often, a **proverb** does not say directly what it means, but uses an example as a symbol. The proverb **"Small strokes fell great oaks"** creates a mental picture of someone chopping down a huge oak tree. Benjamin Franklin, the American who first published this proverb, wasn't talking about trees. Instead, he was saying that a big task is best completed by breaking it down into little parts.

In *Poor Richard's Almanack*, Franklin also wrote **"A stitch in time saves nine."** Picture a shirt with a tear in the sleeve. If you fix the hole right away it might take only one or two stitches; but if you wait, the hole may get bigger, and you will need to use many more stitches.

Some proverbs use observations about nature to make a point. "Birds of a feather," or birds of the same kind, such as crows or cardinals, do tend to stay together. **"Birds of a feather flock together"** can refer to groups of people who are alike in some way. **"Great oaks from little acorns grow"** is another observation that expresses a truth about life: small things can grow into large, important things.

Proverbs may offer practical advice, such as **"Don't judge a book by its cover."** A book with an exciting cover can turn out to be dull and boring. Likewise, a person who appears happy may really be sad inside. **"Look before you leap"** is a bit of practical advice that can be applied to many situations. Just as you wouldn't leap over a fence without checking what's on the other side, you shouldn't take an action without considering what may result. In Franklin's proverb, **"Never leave till tomorrow that which you can do today,"** Franklin used "today" to mean "as soon as possible." His advice to you would be to do your homework as soon as you get it!

1. Which two proverbs use trees as symbols?

   _____

2. Choose two proverbs to encourage someone to start projects now rather than later. Circle them in the passage and explain your choices.

   _____

   _____

> ## *Proverbs*
>
> **Don't judge a book by its cover.**
>
> **Never leave till tomorrow that which you can do today.**
>
> **Birds of a feather flock together.**
>
> **Small strokes fell great oaks.**
>
> **Look before you leap.**
>
> **Great oaks from little acorns grow.**
>
> **A stitch in time saves nine.**

C Write the proverb that best fits each example.

1. Forming an opinion of people by how they are dressed is not a good idea. For this reason, we say _____

2. Have you ever noticed how people who like sports always seem to spend a lot of time together? This is what is meant by _____ _____

3. When we realized that the huge company had started in the owner's garage, we thought _____

4. Your teacher assigned a project to be done over a week's vacation. It is Sunday night and you haven't started yet. If only someone had said to you: _____

5. Evan's room was a mess. It would be a big job to clean. The desk was covered with books and papers. Sports equipment was falling out of the closet. He would have to break the job apart and do a little at a time.

   _____

6. A truth about life that is expressed in a sentence containing symbols is called a _____ .

D   Describe a situation in which you might use each proverb.

1. Look before you leap.

   _____

   _____

2. Birds of a feather flock together.

   _____

   _____

3. Don't judge a book by its cover.

   _____

   _____

4. A stitch in time saves nine.

   _____

   _____

ENRICHMENT

1. **Beware of a wolf in sheep's clothing** *means watch out for people who seem friendly and harmless. They may actually intend to harm you.*

2. **The pen is mightier than the sword** *means people can be more truly conquered by persuasive words than by force.*

OFF THE PAGE

Make a poster for one of the proverbs in this lesson or one that you know. Illustrate the proverb exactly, but explain what the proverb really means. For example, on a poster for "A stitch in time saves nine," you might show a person sewing. Then you would add an explanation of the real meaning.

Review
Lessons 21-24

In this lesson, you will review the words and skills you have learned in the last four lessons. This will help you to remember them when you read and write.

 MATCHING WORDS AND DEFINITIONS Write the word from the box that matches each definition.

| proverb academic odyssey stubborn youthful reckless immature fearless |

1. young and energetic _____
2. not willing to change _____
3. taking stupid risks _____
4. having to do with school _____
5. wise saying _____
6. brave _____
7. long, adventurous journey _____
8. childish _____

 USING WORDS IN CONTEXT Use the words in the box to complete the paragraph.

| panic   mentor   Herculean   colossal   odyssey   skeptical |

   What began as a short trip to visit a favorite teacher, ended up being a month-long **(1)** _____ for Angela and Corinne. They had been in a **(2)** _____ because their community center did not have enough money to rent a bus for a field trip. With the advice of their **(3)** _____ , Mr. Fukushima, however, they were soon on their way. He suggested they hold a car wash to raise money. At first Corinne was **(4)** _____ about the plan, but Angela soon convinced her it would work. It did seem like the fundraiser would take a **(5)** _____ effort, Angela agreed, but she thought they could do it. Sure enough, with Mr. Fukushima's help, the car wash was held within the month and was a **(6)** _____ success!

PRACTICING PROVERBS Choose the saying from the box that best matches each situation. Write it in the space provided.

> **Don't judge a book by its cover.**
>
> **Great oaks from little acorns grow.**
>
> **A stitch in time saves nine.**
>
> **Look before you leap.**
>
> **Never leave till tomorrow that which you can do today.**

1. Everyone at the recital was amazed at how well Daniel played his piano piece. They all remembered that just two years ago he barely knew where to put his fingers.

   Saying: _____

   _____

2. Mercedes was surprised to find that her birthday present was a beautiful, hand-painted ornament. She had not expected much because the gift box had been wrapped in plain, brown paper.

   Saying: _____

   _____

3. Nothing could be done about it. Jennifer had put all her money in the vending machine without bothering to read the "out of order" sign.

   Saying: _____

   _____

4. Camila decided to R.S.V.P. to the party right away.

   Saying: _____

   _____

5. Putting tape around the weak parts of the splintery, old broom was a good idea. By doing that, Clarice was making sure it wouldn't break later—or give her a splinter—when she used it to sweep up the yard for the party.

   Saying: _____

   _____

D **SHADES OF MEANING** This exercise helps you review the different shades of meaning in words. Remember that shades of meaning were discussed in Lesson 21 and in Lesson 22. Read each paragraph. Write the correct word in the blank to complete the sentence.

1. Shira always noticed the smallest details. When she went to visit her grandparents, she said, "Wow, you changed the furniture in the living room!" When she came back home, she noticed that her parents had gotten a new mailbox.

   The best word to describe Shira is _____ .
   (observant/prying)

2. There was a lot of tension during the last game of the all-city basketball finals. The Tigers finally won by a two-point margin in overtime. After the game, to everyone's amazement, Tim, the center on the losing team, lay down on the gym floor and threw a tantrum.

   The best word to describe Tim is _____ .
   (youthful/immature)

3. The accident could have been avoided. Evidently, Joanne and Michael were having a contest as to who could bring their dirty dishes fastest to the dish-washing station in the cafeteria. That's when they ran into each other, breaking many dishes, as well as causing a few bruises.

   The best word to describe Joanne and Michael is _____ .
   (fearless/reckless)

4. Everyone had agreed to the plan except Jill. Each player would take a turn at bat and then pitch the ball to the next batter. For some reason, Jill wouldn't go along. "I just don't feel like it," she whined.

   The best word to describe Jill is _____ .
   (determined/stubborn)

TEST-TAKING STRATEGIES Some **analogies** have word pairs that are synonyms. Some analogies have word pairs that are antonyms. Others go together in a "someone who" or "something that" relationship.

Strategy: Some analogy test items have a blank somewhere other than at the end. You use the same strategy to figure out the answer.

> human : mortal :: _____ : immortal
>
> (A) man   (B) woman   (C) Greek   (D) god

Read this item as, "A human is someone who is mortal and 'blank' is someone who is immortal." Choose the word that makes sense. (god)

Directions: Fill in the bubble next to the word that fits in each analogy.

1. busybody : prying : : _____ : observant
   (A) scientist   (B) microscope   (C) grandfather   (D) academic

2. stubborn : determined :: : _____ : thin
   (A) plump   (B) fearless   (C) well-fed   (D) emaciated

3. doubtful : skeptical : : _____ : panicky
   (A) Herculean (B) wonderful   (C) risky   (D) fearful

4. father : parent : : _____ : advisor
   (A) hospital   (B) mentor   (C) school   (D) odyssey

5. colossal : tiny : : _____ : reckless
   (A) careful   (B) huge   (C) foolish   (D) neat

ENRICHMENT WORDS

> Draw a line between each Enrichment Word and its definition.
>
> 1. drudge   lacking in comfort
> 2. Spartan   a learned person
> 3. scholar   one who works hard at doing
>   boring work
> 4. chaos   confusion
> 5. Beware of a wolf in   Written words are more effective
>   sheep's clothing.   than fighting.
> 6. The pen is mightier   Watch out for people who seem
>   than the sword.   friendly and harmless.

LOOKING INTO WORDS

Skill Lesson
prefixes, suffixes, and roots

A **PREFIXES, SUFFIXES, ROOTS** Three word parts that help you with meaning are **prefix**, **root**, and **suffix**. A **prefix** comes before a root and affects its meaning. A **root** is the main meaning of the word. Some roots are words and some are not. A **suffix** comes after a root and often changes the number, tense, or part of speech of a word.

The word **disconnecting** has a prefix, a root that is a word, and a suffix. Look for the dashes that show where the prefix and suffix attach to the word.

> prefix **dis-**   root **connect**   suffix **-ing**

disconnecting

The word **distracted** has a prefix, a root that is *not* a word, and a suffix. Again, look for the dashes. Notice that the root, **tract,** cannot stand alone as a word.

> prefix **dis-**   root **tract**   suffix **-ed**

Now let's practice dividing words into prefixes, roots, and suffixes. Write the prefix, root, and suffix for the words below. In this exercise, all the roots are words. Remember to use dashes in the right place. The first one has been done for you.

WORD	PREFIX	ROOT	SUFFIX
disarrangement	dis-	arrange	-ment
disappearance			
transplanting			
dishonesty			
amphitheaters			

PREFIXES In the next three lessons, you will be learning more prefixes. These prefixes and their meanings are listed below.

Prefix	Meaning
dis-	opposite, not
trans-	across, go across
ambi-, *amphi-*	both, around
circu-	around

Now try some examples with *dis-*. Write the meaning of the prefix in each blank.

1. *Disorder* means _____ order.

2. *Discomfort* means _____ comfort.

3. *Dishonesty* means _____ honesty.

The above examples were fairly simple to figure out because the roots were words. But sometimes a root that is *not* a word is used. In this case, you can still use the prefix—along with the context—to help you understand the meaning of an unknown word. For example, look at the word *disturb* in the following sentence.

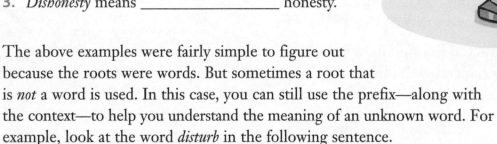

The noise of the bulldozer working next door gradually began to <u>disturb</u> Harry's sleep.

You do not have to know the meaning of the root *turb* to understand that Harry could not continue sleeping.

 PREFIX *TRANS-* Now try some examples with *trans-*. Write the meaning of the prefix ("across" or "go across") in the blanks below.

1. The **transcontinental** railroad reaches _____ the continent.

2. A radio **transmission** travels _____ the air waves to a receiver.

3. An airplane flight that _____ an ocean is called **transoceanic**.

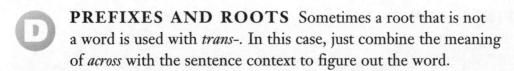

D **PREFIXES AND ROOTS** Sometimes a root that is not a word is used with *trans-*. In this case, just combine the meaning of *across* with the sentence context to figure out the word.

> **Translate** means to express in a different language, or to go "across" languages.
>
> **Transfer** means to move from one place to another, or to go "across" places.
>
> A **transplant** takes something from one place and plants, or puts it, somewhere else, or "across" places.

At times, rather than meaning *across*, the prefix *trans-* may include the idea of movement or change. In the word **transform,** for example, we change forms, or "move across" forms. In the following examples, use your knowledge of the prefix *trans-*, along with the context and your common sense, to figure out the meaning of the boldfaced words.

1. After emerging from the cocoon, it was obvious that the caterpillar had

   been **transformed** into a butterfly.

   Transformed means _____ .

2. After losing so much blood in the car accident, the patient needed a

   blood **transfusion.**

   Transfusion means _____ .

3. Trains, trucks, ships, and airplanes are all ways to **transport** goods to

   stores.

   Transport means _____ .

PREFIXES *AMBI-* AND *AMPHI-* Some prefixes have more than one meaning. *Ambi-* and *amphi-* may mean "both" or "around." When you come upon a new word with the prefix *ambi-* or *amphi-*, for example, you may have to try out both meanings to see which makes the most sense. Once again, you can use context clues and your common sense. In each sentence below, write *both* or *around* to complete the sentence.

1. Someone who is **ambidextrous** can write equally well with

   _____ hands.

2. **Amphibians** are animals that live _____ on land and

   in water.

3. To **amble** from place to place is to walk _____ slowly.

4. An **amphitheater** has rows of seats rising _____ an

   open space at the center.

 WORD PART *CIRCU-* In these words, *circu-* means "around." *Circu-* is usually a prefix. Sometimes it is a root, as it is in the word *encircle.*

1. Your **circulatory system** pumps blood _____ your

   body.

2. **Circumlocution** is talking _____ a topic, but never

   getting to the point.

3. To **circumnavigate** the globe is to sail _____ the world.

4. To **circumvent** the law is to try to get _____ it.

circumnavigate

Opposite "Dis-"
prefix dis-

disaster

A The prefix *dis-* means "not" or "opposite." The words below all include this prefix. You will find this prefix in many words, so studying words with *dis-* will help you in reading and writing.

1. **disadvantage** (dĭs' əd văn' tĭj)
A **disadvantage** *is an unfavorable condition; a condition that makes something harder.* (noun)
It can be a **disadvantage** to be short if you want to be a basketball star.

2. **disagreeable** (dĭs' ə grē' ə bəl)
Something **disagreeable** *is unpleasant.* (adjective)
Skunks produce a very **disagreeable** odor when they are frightened.

3. **disaster** (dĭ zăs' tər) *A* **disaster** *is a calamity or terrible event that causes suffering.* (noun)
The sinking of the *Titanic* was a **disaster** that killed many people.

4. **discharge** (dĭs chärj') *To* **discharge** *is to release, get rid of, or send away.* (verb)
Doctors will **discharge** the patient from the hospital two days after the operation.

5. **discomfort** (dĭs kŭm' fərt)
Discomfort *is the opposite of comfort or ease.* (noun)
The hard, lumpy seats caused great **discomfort** for the audience.

6. **discontent** (dĭs' kən tĕnt')
Discontent *is a feeling of not being happy or satisfied.* (noun)
Students voiced their **discontent** with the long lines in the school cafeteria.

7. **discouraged** (dĭ skûr' ĭjd)
When people become **discouraged,** *they lose hope or confidence.* (adjective)
When she saw how fast her opponents ran, Marla became **discouraged** and quit the race.

8. **disgrace** (dĭs grās') *A* **disgrace** *is a loss of honor or respect; a disgrace brings shame.* (noun)
The mayor left office in **disgrace** when he was found guilty of stealing city money.

Draw a line between each vocabulary word and its definition.

1. disgrace   terrible event

2. discharge   lack of ease

3. discomfort   unpleasant

4. disaster   shame

5. disagreeable   release

All the boldfaced words in the passage below include the prefix *dis-*.
Read the passage. Then answer the questions that follow.

Stagecoaches: Romance or Discomfort?

Does traveling by stagecoach sound exciting to you? During the 1800s, stagecoaches carried passengers to the West. With luck, a trip from Missouri to California took twenty days. Inside the stagecoach, six passengers sat on benches. On long trips, a passenger might be stuck next to a boring or **disagreeable** person for several days.

As the coach swayed back and forth, people often experienced the **discomfort** of motion sickness. In spring and fall, coaches rode through mud. In winter, the uneven frozen tracks bounced passengers several feet into the air.

Many stagecoaches traveled day and night. It was difficult for people to sleep because of the big bounces on rough dirt roads. If a coach was stuck in mud, the passengers had to get out and push. If horses were injured, someone walked to the nearest stagecoach station for help. **Disaster** was always possible.

A few coaches went off cliffs in the dark of night. Others were robbed.

The coach stopped for meals, but passengers often had to eat very quickly. Naturally, this led to much **discontent.** Some passengers became **discouraged** about completing the trip. When the coach **discharged** passengers for dinner, they might decide not to get back on.

In contrast, the drivers were tough and determined. They considered it a personal **disgrace** if their stagecoaches did not finish the trip safely. Yet, as hard as they tried, it was difficult to go more than fifteen miles per hour.

With all of these **disadvantages,** people were anxious for other ways to get to the West. As the railroads reached more areas, stagecoaches rapidly disappeared.

WORD LIST

disadvantage

disagreeable

disaster

discharge

discomfort

discontent

discouraged

disgrace

1. What was it like to travel by stagecoach? Use at least two vocabulary words in your answer. _____

_____

2. What were two of the disasters that could happen during stagecoach travel? _____

_____

C Underline the word in each row that is a synonym for the boldfaced word.

1. **discontent**   joy   unhappiness   fear

2. **disgrace**   honor   bore   shame

3. **discharge**   release   welcome   bring

4. **disagreeable**   fun   unpleasant   correct

5. **disaster**   flower   destination   tragedy

D Remember that *dis-* means "opposite." Fill in the blanks below by choosing the correct word. This exercise will help you to understand the prefix *dis-* and how it is used with roots.

1. An **agreeable** person is easy to get along with. A **disagreeable** person is the _____ *(opposite/across)*. Here *dis-* is a _____ *(suffix/prefix)* that is added to the root **agreeable.**

2. A person who is **encouraged** thinks good things will happen. A person who is **discouraged** thinks _____ *(good/bad)* things will happen. An **encouraged** person could be said to be "filled with" courage. A **discouraged** person could be said to be _____ *(emptied of/helped by)* courage.

3. The ancient Greeks felt that the stars brought good luck. Their word for stars sounded like *aster*. In the word **disaster,** the prefix is _____ *(dis-/aster)*. The prefix plus the root mean "the _____ *(same as/opposite of)* good luck."

OTHER FORMS

disadvantageous

disagreeably

disagreement

discomforting

discontentment

disgraceful

disgracefully

E Complete each sentence with a phrase that fits. Note that some other forms of the vocabulary words have been used.

1. **Discontentment** can lead to _____

_____ .

2. Something that causes great **discomfort** is _____

_____ .

3. It's **disgraceful** to _____

_____ .

4. When you feel **discouraged,** _____

_____ .

5. An example of a **disagreeable** sight is _____

_____ .

ENRICHMENT WORDS

Here are two more words that have the prefix *dis-*.

1. **disintegrate** (dĭs ĭn' tĭ grāt') *To* **disintegrate** *is to fall apart or become worse; the opposite of integrate.* (verb)

   Old paper can **disintegrate** into powder if it becomes too dry.

2. **disclose** (dĭs klōz') *To* **disclose** *means to let out a secret or to uncover.* (verb)

   Tomorrow, the judges will **disclose** who won the contest.

OFF THE PAGE

Choose two vocabulary words from the lesson. First use each word in a sentence. Then take off the prefix *dis-* and use the remaining words in their own sentences. Here's an example.

The smell of trash can be disagreeable.

The smell of cooking food can be agreeable.

Across the Way
prefix trans-

A The prefix *trans-* means "across" or "go across." At times it can also mean "movement" or "change." The words below all include *trans-*. Try to figure out what *trans-* means in each word.

1. **transaction** (trăn săk' shən) *A* **transaction** *is an act, especially business, done between, or "across," people.* (noun) The **transaction** was complete when both parties signed the documents.

2. **transcontinental** (trăns' kŏn tə **nĕn'** tl) **Transcontinental** *means crossing a continent.* (adjective) We took a **transcontinental** flight from Los Angeles to New York.

3. **transform** (trăns fôrm') *To* **transform** *something is to change its form or appearance.* (verb) It's exciting to see a tadpole **transform** into a frog.

4. **transfusion** (trăns fyoo' zhən) *A* **transfusion** *is the transfer of something, such as blood, from one person or thing into another.* (noun) Before you receive a **transfusion** of blood, check your blood type.

5. **transition** (trăn zĭsh' ən) *A* **transition** *is the process of passing, or going across, from one activity or place to another.* (noun) Serena made the **transition** from her old school to her new one easily.

6. **translate** (trăns' lāt') *To* **translate** *means to take something from one language and express it in another.* (verb) My grandmother speaks only Greek, so I **translate** her words into English for my friends.

7. **transplant** (trăns plant') *To* **transplant** *is to move something that is planted in one place to another place.* (verb) We decided to **transplant** the rose bush from our old house to our new house.

8. **transport** (trăns pôrt') *To* **transport** *means to carry something from one place to another.* (verb) The truck driver will **transport** the peaches from South Carolina to New York.

Draw a line between each vocabulary word and its definition.

1. transport — express in another language

2. transplant — from one activity to another

3. translate — carry from one place to another

4. transition — uproot and plant elsewhere

The boldfaced words in the passage below all contain the prefix *trans-*. Read the passage. Then answer the questions that follow.

Transplants: Modern Medical Miracle

Just fifty years ago, a child with inherited lung or kidney disease would probably have died before reaching adulthood. But today, we can **transplant** organs from one person to another and save many lives. A precious organ may even make a **transcontinental** journey to reach the person who needs it.

Suffering from cystic-fibrosis, teenager Andrew Croy waited for new lungs. Armed with a pager, he was ready to go into surgery at a moment's notice. Finally, a national network found a donor's lungs and called Andrew's hospital. If Andrew did not accept the donation within one hour, the lungs would have to be given to someone else. The hospital paged Andrew only to find that his beeper was out of order! Frantically, they called his mother, located him at a hockey game, and got him to the hospital with only fifteen minutes to spare. Meanwhile, a medical team flew to the donor's hospital to pick up the lungs and **transport** them to Andrew. Soon, Andrew was on the operating table, with blood supplies ready in case a **transfusion** was needed. The entire **transaction** took only a few hours. Today, Andrew's life has been **transformed** by his new, healthy lungs. He now can live normally, without fear of life-threatening infection.

Transplants have saved thousands of lives. Like Andrew, many people have been able to make the **transition** from illness back to health. In today's world, a person's signature on a card that allows organs to be given to another person **translates** into the gift of life.

1. How was Croy's life transformed by the operation?

   _____

   _____

2. Explain how each of the three words below are involved when a doctor transfers an organ from one person to another: **transport, transplant, transfusion.**

   _____

   _____

WORD LIST

transaction

transcontinental

transform

transfusion

transition

translate

transplant

transport

C Choose the vocabulary word that best completes each sentence. Write the word on the line.

1. We took a _____ flight from Morocco in northern Africa to South Africa. *(transcontinental/transform/transfusion)*

2. It's difficult to _____ large packages on a bicycle. *(translate/transition/transport)*

3. I'm planning to _____ this piece of junk into a work of art. *(transport/transaction/transform)*

4. When you _____ a rose bush, put a banana peel in the new hole to give the plant extra potassium and improve its growth. *(transplant/transaction/transition)*

5. When you _____ from one language to another, you need to be careful to keep the original sense of what was said. *(transfusion/transport/translate)*

D Remember that *trans-* usually means "across" or "go across." At times it can also mean "movement" or "change." Fill in the blanks below by choosing the correct choice.

1. A **transaction** is an action that goes _____ *(opposite/across)* people. The root in this word is _____ *(action/trans-)*.

2. When we **transform** something, we _____ *(around/change)* it from one form to another. In this word, the root _____ *(is/is not)* a word.

3. When we **translate** something, it goes _____ *(across/opposite)* languages. We know this because the _____ *(prefix/suffix)* is *trans-*.

transaction

OTHER FORMS

transact

transformation

transfuse

translation

translator

transportation

E Complete each sentence with a phrase that makes sense. Note that some other forms of the vocabulary words are used.

1. My favorite form of **transportation** is _____
_____ .

2. A person might need a **transfusion** if _____
_____ .

3. I would like to **transform** the playground into _____
_____ .

4. The **transition** from our old house to our new house _____
_____ .

5. The job of a **translator** might be to _____
_____ .

ENRICHMENT WORDS

Here are two more words that begin with the prefix *trans-*. How many other words can you list?

1. **transitory** (tran' si tôr' e) *Something that is* **transitory** *lasts for only a short time; it passes quickly.* (adjective)

   Maria's wish for a dog was **transitory;** the next week she wanted a cat.

2. **transpose** (trans pōz') *When we* **transpose** *things, we reverse their positions.* (verb)

   I accidentally **transposed** 43 by writing it as 34.

transcontinental

OFF THE PAGE

Write about a transcontinental trip you might take. You may choose to cross any of the seven continents. Be specific about where you will go, how you will travel, and what sights you will see.

Around and Around
word parts ambi-, amphi-, circu-

A The prefixes *ambi-* and *amphi-* mean "both" or "around." *Circu-* means "around." The words below include these word parts. As you study the words, think about what the word part means in each one.

1. **ambition** (ăm bĭsh' ən) **Ambition** *is a desire to achieve or do something.* (noun).
His **ambition** to become a pilot led him to take flying lessons.

2. **amble** (ăm' bəl) *To* **amble** *is to walk around slowly.* (verb)
We like to **amble** through the park, enjoying the trees.

3. **amphibian** (ăm fĭb' ē ən) **An amphibian** *is an animal that lives both on land and in water.* (noun)
A frog is an example of an **amphibian.**

4. **circuitous** (sər kyōō' ĭ təs)
A **circuitous** *route is not direct, but is roundabout.* (adjective)
Since Tom wasn't in a hurry to get to school, he took a **circuitous** route, stopping at several places that were out of the way.

5. **circulate** (sûr' kyĕ lāt) *To* **circulate** *is to move around in a circle.* (verb)
Blood **circulates** through the human body, supplying it with oxygen.

6. **circumference** (sər kŭm' fər əns)
The **circumference** *is the distance around a circle.* (noun)
The **circumference** of the earth is about 25,000 miles.

7. **cycle** (sī' kəl) *A* **cycle** *is a series of events that repeats, or goes around, many times.* (noun)
The **cycle** of seasons—winter, spring, summer, and fall—repeats each year.

8. **encircle** (ĕn sûr' kəl) *To* **encircle** *is to put a circle around.* (verb)
To protect their camp, the settlers would **encircle** it with their wagons.

Draw a line between each vocabulary word and its definition.

1. circulate — strong desire
2. encircle — repetition of events
3. ambition — move around
4. cycle — put a circle around
5. circuitous — lives both on land and in water
6. amphibian — not direct

circumference

The boldfaced words in the passage below have the word parts *ambi-*, *amphi-*, or *circu-*. Read the passage. Then answer the questions that follow.

Croaking Frogs Mean a Healthy Environment

Three times each year, a group of people from Chicago follow a **circuitous** path through parks, lawns, and roadsides. As they go, they listen for the sounds of frogs. Their **ambition** is to count and classify each one. As they **amble** around the **circumference** of a park, they might hear the musical trill of an American frog or the deep croak of a bull frog. More croaks mean more frogs.

In recent years, scientists have noted a steep decrease in the number of frogs and other **amphibians** such as toads, salamanders, and newts. This may be an early warning of trouble in the environment. Amphibians are very sensitive to environmental changes.

What could be going wrong? One problem may be a thinning of the ozone layer that **encircles** the earth. The thinner layer lets in too much ultra-violet light for frog eggs. This kills the frog at the earliest part of its life **cycle.** Researchers found that eggs protected from the sun's rays hatched much better than unprotected eggs.

Another problem may be a newly discovered virus, found on the skin of frogs. Strangely, this may be caused by human beings who are trying to protect frogs. As scientists **circulate** through frog habitats in an effort to study them, they may be accidentally spreading the virus.

Whatever the cause, we need to protect the world's frogs. Across the world, volunteers and professionals are listening to frog croaks and researching ways to help this precious part of the environment.

WORD LIST

ambition

amble

amphibian

circuitous

circulate

circumference

cycle

encircle

1. Describe one change that could be affecting the amphibian population.

_____

_____

2. Why do the people follow a circuitous route?

_____

_____

C Circle the word that best completes each sentence.

1. Let's (*encircle*   *circulate*   *amble*) down to the river bank.

2. To secure the back yard, (*cycle*   *encircle*   *ambition*) it with a fence.

3. Elena's (*amphibian*   *ambition*   *cycle*) is to become a doctor.

4. (*Circuitous*   *Circumference*   *Encircle*) is the opposite of *direct*.

5. A(n) (*amphibian*   *ambition*   *circumference*) is a cold-blooded animal.

D *Ambi-* and *amphi-* mean "both" or "around." *Circum-* means "around." Fill in the blanks below by choosing the correct word or phrase.

1. In the word **circumference** the prefix *circum-* means _____ (*around/both*). The root *ference* _____ (*is/is not*) a word. In the word **amphibian,** the prefix *amphi-* means _____ (*around/both*).

2. At times, a word part changes its spelling when it is put into a word. The words **cycle** and **encircle** contain the word part _____ (*ambi-/circum-*), but it is spelled differently in these words. When *circum-* is used as the prefix of the word, it comes _____ (*before/after*) a root.

3. In ancient Rome, people who wanted to be elected for an office were called **ambitious** because they went _____ (*around/both*) the town looking for votes.

E Complete each sentence with a phrase that fits. Note that other forms of the vocabulary words are used in some sentences.

1. Someone who is **ambitious** _____

_____ .

2. An example of an **amphibious** animal is _____

_____ .

3. When you **recycle,** _____

_____ .

4. A fan **circulates** air by _____

_____ .

5. If you **amble** along, you _____

_____ .

ENRICHMENT WORDS

Here are two more words that use the word parts *ambi-* and *circum-*. Do you know anyone who is ambidextrous?

1. **ambidextrous** (am' bi **dek**' strəs) *An* **ambidextrous** *person can use right and left hands equally well.* (adjective)

   In 1995, **ambidextrous** baseball player Greg Harris used both his right hand and his left hand to pitch in the same game.

2. **circumvent** (sûr' kəm **vent**') *When we* **circumvent** *something, we avoid it or go around it.* (verb)

   Some people use e-mail to **circumvent** the problem of slow mail delivery.

OFF THE PAGE

Do a word web for the word **cycle.** Write the word *cycle* in the middle of a piece of paper. Circle it. All around the circle, write words that have the word *cycle* as the root. List at least four words besides *recycle.* Use a dictionary, if you wish.

recycle

cycle

Review
Lessons 26–29

In this lesson, you will review the words and skills you
have learned in the last four lessons. This will help
you to remember them when you read and write.

A **MATCHING WORDS AND DEFINITIONS**
Write the word from the box that matches each definition.

cycle	discouraged	transaction	encircle	disgrace
	ambition	transition	discharge	

1. loss of honor or respect _____

2. desire to achieve or do something _____

3. carrying out a business action between people _____

4. passage from one activity to another _____

5. a series of events that repeats _____

6. to put a circle around _____

7. without hope or confidence _____

8. to release or send away _____

B **USING WORDS IN CONTEXT** Use the words in the
box to complete the paragraph.

transporting	circuitous	discomfort	circulate	disaster	disagreeable

The Sanchez family vacation had nearly been a **(1)** _____ .
All they wanted to do was attend a reunion with their relatives in Juarez,
Mexico. Because they were **(2)** _____ a great deal of
luggage and many gifts, they decided to rent a van to take them over the
border. But the closing of roads for construction forced them to take a
(3) _____ route to their destination. This made the trip
take several hours longer than usual. It wasn't until they were well on their
way that they discovered that the air conditioning in the rented van didn't
work properly. The air was still and didn't **(4)** _____ at all.

This caused a great deal of **(5)** _____ as they traveled

through the hot, dry countryside. But once they arrived at the reunion,

their experience was far from **(6)** _____ .

C **WRITING SENTENCES** Choose two of the words on each line to use in a sentence. You can change the form of the word if you like. (For example, *transport* may be changed to *transportation*, or *circuitous* may be changed to *circuitously*.)

1. **transport   cycle   disaster**

_____

_____

2. **circuitous   discontent   amble**

_____

_____

3. **transplant   circumference   transition**

_____

_____

4. **ambition   disgrace   transform**

_____

_____

D **UNDERSTANDING THE WORDS** Answer the following questions. Use the boldfaced word in your answer.

1. When would someone need a **transfusion?**

_____

_____

2. What do you know about **amphibians?**

_____

_____

3. What **disadvantages** do people have without a good education?

_____

_____

4. What sights would you see on a **transcontinental** car trip from California to Florida?

_____

_____

5. What would you say to someone who was **discouraged** because her favorite team lost the championship?

_____

_____

E **TEST-TAKING STRATEGIES** To solve an **analogy,** you need to have the two word pairs related in the same way.

Strategy: Remember that there are different kinds of relationships that an analogy can have. Some of them are synonyms, antonyms, "someone who is" or "something that is," and "type of."

oak : tree :: _____ : building
(A) plant   (B) shed   (C) maple   (D) carpenter

An oak is a type of tree, so read this analogy as, "Oak is a type of tree, and 'blank' is a type of building." Then look for the word that fits in the analogy. (A shed is a type of building.)

Directions: Fill in the bubble next to the word that fits in each analogy.

1. disagreeable : agreeable : : _____ : advantage
   (A) friendly   (B) disadvantage (C) discharge   (D) discourage

2. wolf : vertebrate : : frog : _____
   (A) mammal   (B) toad   (C) backbone   (D) amphibian

3. change : transform : : _____ : discontent
   (A) content   (B) alter   (C) unhappiness   (D) discomfort

(continued)

4. walk : amble : : _____ : dim

(A) light bulb   (B) fast   (C) around   (D) gloomy

5. disgrace : honor : : _____ : circuitous

(A) encircle   (B) direct   (C) dishonor   (D) round

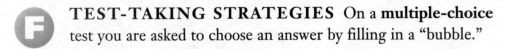

F **TEST-TAKING STRATEGIES** On a **multiple-choice** test you are asked to choose an answer by filling in a "bubble."

Strategy: Read the test item with the answer in place to see if you are correct *before* you fill in the bubble.

Directions: Fill in the bubble next to the word or phrase that gives the meaning of the underlined word part.

1. <u>circ</u>ulate   en<u>circ</u>le

(A) around   (B) across   (C) opposite   (D) change

2. <u>trans</u>fusion   <u>trans</u>mitter

(A) opposite   (B) across   (C) around   (D) both

3. <u>dis</u>aster   <u>dis</u>content

(A) around   (B) across   (C) both of   (D) opposite

4. <u>amb</u>le   <u>amb</u>itheater

(A) across   (B) both   (C) opposite   (D) around

5. <u>trans</u>polar   <u>trans</u>port

(A) opposite   (B) across   (C) absence   (D) both

ENRICHMENT WORDS

Draw a line between each Enrichment Word and its definition.

1. transitory   able to use both hands

2. transpose   go around

3. ambidextrous   fall apart

4. circumvent   lasts a short time

5. disintegrate   let out a secret or uncover

6. disclose   reverse position

Word List for Grade 5

abolish	45	discouraged	105	magnificent	25	Spartan (E)	92
academic	89	disgrace	105	maneuver (E)	32	species	49
acute	49	disintegrate (E)	108	marvel	29	spotless	5
ambidextrous (E)	116	dormant (E)	52	medium (E)	36	stealthily	25
ambition	113	drudge (E)	88	mentor	89	stubborn	85
amble	113	dusk	13	Midas touch	89	subculture (E)	68
amphibian	113	elaborate	5	mortal	53	submarine	65
appointed	45	elected	45	myth	53	submerged	65
apprentice	45	emaciated	5	nomad	25	subservient	65
arm	33	encircle	113	nimble (E)	28	subterranean	65
auditory	49	enclose	25	nutritious (E)	52	subzero	65
bicentennial	73	exquisite	5	observant	85	superabundant (E)	68
bilingual (E)	76	fate	53	odious	9	superfluous	65
biped	73	fearless	85	odyssey	89	superheated	65
brawny (E)	8	feast	29	olfactory	49	superimposed	65
candid (E)	12	fool	29	Olympian (E)	56	tactile	49
carriage	45	fragile	5	optimistic (E)	12	tattered	5
chaos (E)	92	frustrated	9	panic	89	timeless	53
charge	33	gloomy	13	plaza	13	transaction	109
circuitous	113	gorge	33	plea	25	transcontinental	109
circulate	113	guarantee	29	predator	49	transform	109
circumference	113	hamlet	13	proclamation (E)	48	transfusion	109
circumvent (E)	116	Herculean	89	prosperous	45	transition	109
colossal	89	homely	5	proverb	93	transitory (E)	112
commonplace	25	honorable	9	prying	85	translate	109
congested (E)	16	illegal	69	psyche	53	transplant	109
convene (E)	48	ill-informed	9	ravine	13	transport	109
counter (E)	36	illogical	69	realm	53	transpose (E)	112
cycle	113	immature	85	rebellion	45	triathlon (E)	76
dash	33	immodest	69	rebuke (E)	32	trilogy	73
deity (E)	56	immortal	53	reckless	85	triple	73
depression	33	immovable	69	representative	45	trivial	73
desperate	9	immune	69	responsive	49	unicellular	73
determined	85	imperfection	69	roam	25	unique	73
dilapidated (E)	16	impersonal (E)	72	roll	33	universe	73
din (E)	28	improper	69	ruefully	25	vegetation	13
disadvantage	105	intolerable	69	scholar (E)	88	vertebrate	49
disagreeable	105	invariably (E)	72	scout	29	vow	29
disaster	105	invincible	53	shiver	29	well-informed	9
discharge	105	lanky	5	shrewd	9	wrench	29
disclose (E)	108	lithe (E)	8	skeptical	89	yarn	33
discomfort	105	looming	13	skirt	33	youthful	85
discontent	105	lush	13	solemn	9		

(E) = Enrichment Words